THE CAMBRIDGE POCKET SHAKESPEARE

General Editor: JOHN DOVER WILSON

KING JOHN

KING JOHN

EDITED BY

JOHN DOVER WILSON

CAMBRIDGE

At the University Press

1958

PUBLISHED BY
THE SYNDICS OF THE CAMBRIDGE UNIVERSITY PRESS

Bentley House, 200 Euston Road, London, N.W. 1
American Branch: 32 East 57th Street, New York 22, N.Y.

First edition (The New Shakespeare)	1936
Reprinted	1954
This edition (The Cambridge Pocket Shakespeare) giving the New Shakespeare text with corrections	1958

*Printed in Great Britain at the University Press, Cambridge
(Brooke Crutchley, University Printer)*

SHAKESPEARE'S PLAYS

This list suggests the order in which most scholars now think the plays were written, and gives approximate dates of composition. Only in a few cases is the issue beyond doubt.

Henry VI, Part I, 1589–90

Henry VI, Parts II and III, 1590–91

Richard III, 1592–93

The Comedy of Errors, 1592–93

Titus Andronicus, 1593–94

The Taming of the Shrew, 1593–94

The Two Gentlemen of Verona, 1594–95

Love's Labour's Lost, 1594–95

Romeo and Juliet, 1595–96

Richard II, 1595–96

A Midsummer Night's Dream, 1595–96

King John, 1596–97

The Merchant of Venice, 1596–97

Henry IV, Parts I and II, 1597–98

Much Ado About Nothing, 1598–99

Henry V, 1598–99

Julius Caesar, 1599–1600

The Merry Wives of Windsor, 1597–1601

As You Like It, 1599–1600

Twelfth Night, 1599–1602

Hamlet, 1600–01

Troilus and Cressida, 1601–02

All's Well that Ends Well, 1602–04

Measure for Measure, 1603–04

Othello, 1603–04

King Lear, 1605–06

Macbeth, 1605–06

Timon of Athens, 1605–08

Antony and Cleopatra, 1606–07

Coriolanus, 1607–08

Pericles, 1608–09

Cymbeline, 1609–10

The Winter's Tale, 1610–11

The Tempest, 1611–12

Henry VIII, 1612–13

An obelisk (†) implies corruption or emendation, a single bracket an aside; single inverted commas are editorial, and mark original stage directions. In plays for which Folio and Quarto texts exist, passages taken from the text not mainly used are enclosed within square brackets. Four dots normally represent a full-stop in the original. Long-armed brackets denote passages either probably not by Shakespeare or later rejected by him.

The Scene: now in England, now in France

CHARACTERS IN THE PLAY

KING JOHN

PRINCE HENRY, *son to the king*

ARTHUR, *Duke of Britain, nephew to the king*

The Earl of Pembroke

The Earl of Essex

The Earl of Salisbury

The Lord BIGOT

HUBERT DE BURGH

ROBERT FAULCONBRIDGE, *son of Sir Robert Faulconbridge*

PHILIP THE BASTARD, *his half-brother*

JAMES GURNEY

PETER *of Pomfret, a prophet*

PHILIP, *King of France*

LEWIS, *the Dauphin*

LYMOGES, *Duke of Austria*

CARDINAL PANDULPH, *the Pope's legate*

MELUN, *a French Lord*

CHATILLION, *ambassador from France to King John*

A Citizen of Angiers

QUEEN ELINOR, *mother to King John*

CONSTANCE, *mother to Arthur*

BLANCH *of Spain, niece to King John*

LADY FAULCONBRIDGE

Lords, Ladies, Citizens of Angiers, Sheriff, Heralds,
  Officers, Soldiers, Messengers, and other Attendants

KING JOHN

England. The palace of KING JOHN

'*Enter KING JOHN, QUEEN ELINOR, PEMBROKE, ESSEX, SALISBURY, with the CHATILLION of France*'. *Attendants.*

K. John. Now, say, Chatillion, what would France
    with us?
Chatillion. Thus, after greeting, speaks the King
    of France
In my behaviour to the majesty,
The borrowed majesty, of England here.
  Elinor. A strange beginning: 'borrowed majesty'!
  K. John. Silence, good mother, hear the embassy.
  Chatillion. Philip of France, in right and true behalf
Of thy deceaséd brother Geffrey's son,
Arthur Plantagenet, lays most lawful claim
To this fair island and the territories,   10
To Ireland, Poictiers, Anjou, Touraine, Maine,
Desiring thee to lay aside the sword
Which sways usurpingly these several titles,
And put the same into young Arthur's hand,
Thy nephew and right royal sovereign.
  K. John. What follows if we disallow of this?
  Chatillion. The proud control of fierce and bloody war,
To enforce these rights so forcibly withheld.
  K. John. Here have we war for war and blood
    for blood,
Controlment for control: so answer France.   20

Chatillion. Then take my king's defiance from
    my mouth,
The farthest limit of my embassy.

    K. John. Bear mine to him, and so depart in peace:
Be thou as lightning in the eyes of France;
For ere thou canst report I will be there,
The thunder of my cannon shall be heard.
So hence! Be thou the trumpet of our wrath,
And sullen presage of your own decay:
An honourable conduct let him have,
30 Pembroke, look to't: farewell, Chatillion.

              [Chatillion and Pembroke depart
    Elinor. What now, my son? have I not ever said
How that ambitious Constance would not cease
Till she had kindled France and all the world,
Upon the right and party of her son?
This might have been prevented and made whole
With very easy arguments of love,
Which now the manage of two kingdoms must
With fearful-bloody issue arbitrate.

    K. John. Our strong possession and our right for us.
40 (*Elinor.* Your strong possession much more than
      your right,
Or else it must go wrong with you and me—
So much my conscience whispers in your ear,
Which none but heaven, and you, and I, shall hear.

    'Enter a Sheriff' and speaks aside with ESSEX

    Essex. My liege, here is the strangest controversy,
Come from the country to be judged by you,
That e'er I heard: shall I produce the men?

    K. John. Let them approach...
Our abbeys and our priories shall pay
This expedition's charge...

*ROBERT FAULCONBRIDGE and PHILIP
his bastard brother enter*

What men are you?

Bastard. Your faithful subject I, a gentleman,   50
Born in Northamptonshire, and eldest son,
As I suppose, to Robert Faulconbridge,
A soldier, by the honour-giving hand
Of Cordelion knighted in the field.

K. John. What art thou?

Robert. The son and heir to that same Faulconbridge.

K. John. Is that the elder, and art thou the heir?
You came not of one mother then, it seems.

Bastard. Most certain of one mother, mighty king—
That is well known—and as I think one father: 60
But for the certain knowledge of that truth
I put you o'er to heaven and to my mother;
Of that I doubt, as all men's children may.

Elinor. Out on thee, rude man! thou dost shame
thy mother,
And wound her honour with this diffidence.

Bastard. I, madam? no, I have no reason for it,
That is my brother's plea and none of mine,
The which if he can prove, a' pops me out
At least from fair five hundred pound a year:
Heaven guard my mother's honour, and my land!   70

K. John. A good blunt fellow...Why, being
younger born,
Doth he lay claim to thine inheritance?

Bastard. I know not why, except to get the land:
But once he slandered me with bastardy:
Now whe'r I be as true begot or no,
That still I lay upon my mother's head,
But that I am as well begot, my liege,

(Fair fall the bones that took the pains for me!)
Compare our faces and be judge yourself.
80 If old Sir Robert did beget us both,
    And were our father, and this son like him,
    O old Sir Robert, father, on my knee
    I give heaven thanks I was not like to thee!
        K. John. Why, what a madcap hath heaven lent us here!
        (*Elinor.* He hath a trick of Cordelion's face,
    The accent of his tongue affecteth him:
    Do you not read some tokens of my son
    In the large composition of this man?
        (*K. John.* Mine eye hath well examinéd his parts,
90 And finds them perfect Richard...[*aloud, to Robert*]
        Sirrah, speak,
    What doth move you to claim your brother's land?
        Bastard. Because he hath a half-face like my father!
    With half that face would he have all my land—
    A half-faced groat five hundred pound a year!
        Robert. My gracious liege, when that my father lived,
    Your brother did employ my father much—
        Bastard. Well, sir, by this you cannot get my land,
    Your tale must be how he employed my mother.
        Robert. And once dispatched him in an embassy
100 To Germany, there with the emperor
    To treat of high affairs touching that time:
    Th' advantage of his absence took the king,
    And in the mean time sojourned at my father's;
    Where how he did prevail I shame to speak,
    But truth is truth: large lengths of seas and shores
    Between my father and my mother lay,
    As I have heard my father speak himself,
    When this same lusty gentleman was got:
    Upon his death-bed he by will bequeathed
110 His lands to me, and took it on his death

That this my mother's son was none of his;
And if he were, he came into the world
Full fourteen weeks before the course of time:
Then, good my liege, let me have what is mine,
My father's land, as was my father's will.

K. John. Sirrah, your brother is legitimate,
Your father's wife did after wedlock bear him:
And if she did play false, the fault was hers,
Which fault lies on the hazards of all husbands
That marry wives: tell me, how if my brother,   120
Who as you say took pains to get this son,
Had of your father claimed this son for his?
In sooth, good friend, your father might have kept
This calf, bred from his cow, from all the world:
In sooth, he might: then, if he were my brother's,
My brother might not claim him, nor your father
Being none of his refuse him: this concludes—
My mother's son did get your father's heir,
Your father's heir must have your father's land.

Robert. Shall then my father's will be of no force   130
To dispossess that child which is not his?

Bastard. Of no more force to dispossess me, sir,
Than was his will to get me, as I think.

Elinor. Whether hadst thou rather be a Faulconbridge,
And like thy brother, to enjoy thy land,
Or the reputed son of Cordelion,
Lord of thy presence and no land beside?

Bastard. Madam, an if my brother had my shape,
And I had his, Sir Robert's his, like him,
And if my legs were two such riding-rods,   140
My arms such eel-skins stuffed, my face so thin
That in mine ear I durst not stick a rose
Lest men should say 'Look, where three-farthings goes!'
And, to his shape, were heir to all this land,

Would I might never stir from off this place,
I would give it every foot to have this face;
I would not be Sir Nob in any case.
    Elinor. I like thee well: wilt thou forsake thy fortune,
Bequeath thy land to him, and follow me?
150 I am a soldier, and now bound to France.
    Bastard. Brother, take you my land, I'll take my chance;
Your face hath got five hundred pound a year,
Yet sell your face for five pence and 'tis dear:
Madam, I'll follow you unto the death.
    Elinor. Nay, I would have you go before me thither.
    Bastard. Our country manners give our betters way.
    K. John. What is thy name?
    Bastard. Philip, my liege, so is my name begun,
Philip, good old Sir Robert's wife's eldest son.
160 *K. John.* From henceforth bear his name whose
        form thou bearest:
Kneel thou down Philip, but rise more great—
Arise Sir Richard, and Plantagenet.
    Bastard. Brother, by th'mother's side, give me
        your hand.
My father gave me honour, yours gave land...
Now blessèd be the hour, by night or day,
When I was got, Sir Robert was away.
    Elinor. The very spirit of Plantagenet!
I am thy grandam, Richard, call me so.
    Bastard. Madam, by chance but not by truth,
        what though?
170 Something about, a little from the right,
    In at the window, or else o'er the hatch:
Who dares not stir by day must walk by night,
    And have is have, however men do catch:
Near or far off, well won is still well shot,
And I am I, howe'er I was begot.

K. John. Go, Faulconbridge, now hast thou
      thy desire,
A landless knight makes thee a landed squire:
Come, madam, and come, Richard, we must speed
For France, for France, for it is more than need.
   Bastard. Brother, adieu, good fortune come to thee! 180
For thou was got i'th' way of honesty....
                         ['*Exeunt all but Bastard*'
A foot of honour better than I was,
But many a many foot of land the worse....
Well, now can I make any Joan a lady.
'Good den, Sir Richard!'—'God-a-mercy, fellow'—
And if his name be George, I'll call him Peter;
For new-made honour doth forget men's names;
'Tis too respective and too sociable
For your conversion. Now your traveller,
He and his toothpick at my worship's mess,   190
And when my knightly stomach is sufficed,
Why then I suck my teeth, and catechize
My pickéd man of countries: 'My dear sir',
Thus leaning on mine elbow I begin,
'I shall beseech you'—that is question now;
And then comes answer like an Absey book:
'O sir,' says answer, 'at your best command,
At your employment, at your service, sir:'
'No, sir,' says question, 'I, sweet sir, at yours.'
And so, ere answer knows what question would,   200
Saving in dialogue of compliment,
And talking of the Alps and Apennines,
The Pyrenean and the river Po,
It draws toward supper in conclusion so....
But this is worshipful society,
And fits the mounting spirit like myself;
For he is but a bastard to the time

That doth not smack of observation.
And so am I, whether I smack or no:
210 And not alone in habit and device,
Exterior form, outward accoutrement;
But from the inward motion to deliver
Sweet, sweet, sweet poison for the age's tooth—
Which, though I will not practise to deceive,
Yet, to avoid deceit, I mean to learn;
For it shall strew the footsteps of my rising...
But who comes in such haste in riding-robes?
What woman-post is this? hath she no husband
That will take pains to blow a horn before her?

'Enter LADY FAULCONBRIDGE and JAMES GURNEY'

220 O me! it is my mother: how now, good lady?
What brings you here to court so hastily?
    Lady Faulconbridge. Where is that slave, thy brother?
        where is he,
That holds in chase mine honour up and down?
    Bastard. My brother Robert? old Sir Robert's son?
Colbrand the giant, that same mighty man?
Is it Sir Robert's son that you seek so?
    Lady Faulconbridge. Sir Robert's son! Ay, thou
        unreverend boy,
Sir Robert's son: why scorn'st thou at Sir Robert?
He is Sir Robert's son, and so art thou.
230 *Bastard.* James Gurney, wilt thou give us leave awhile?
    Gurney. Good leave, good Philip.
    Bastard.   Philip Sparrow, James!
There's toys abroad, anon I'll tell thee more....
                                        [*Gurney goes*
Madam, I was not old Sir Robert's son,
Sir Robert might have eat his part in me
Upon Good-Friday and ne'er broke his fast:
Sir Robert could do well—marry, to confess—

Could he get me. Sir Robert could not do it;
We know his handiwork. Therefore, good mother,
To whom am I beholding for these limbs?
Sir Robert never holp to make this leg.   240
   Lady Faulconbridge. Hast thou conspiréd with thy
       brother too,
That for thine own gain shouldst defend mine honour?
What means this scorn, thou most untoward knave?
   Bastard. Knight, knight, good mother, Basilisco-like:
What! I am dubbed, I have it on my shoulder:
But, mother, I am not Sir Robert's son,
I have disclaimed Sir Robert and my land,
Legitimation, name, and all is gone:
Then, good my mother, let me know my father,
Some proper man I hope, who was it, mother?   250
   Lady Faulconbridge. Hast thou denied thyself
      a Faulconbridge?
   Bastard. As faithfully as I deny the devil.
   Lady Faulconbridge. King Richard Cordelion was
      thy father.
By long and vehement suit I was seduced
To make room for him in my husband's bed:
Heaven lay not my transgression to thy charge,
That art the issue of my dear offence,
Which was so strongly urged past my defence.
   Bastard. Now, by this light, were I to get again,
Madam, I would not wish a better father: 260
Some sins do bear their privilege on earth,
And so doth yours; your fault was not your folly.
Needs must you lay your heart at his dispose,
Subjected tribute to commanding love,
Against whose fury and unmatchéd force
The aweless lion could not wage the fight,
Nor keep his princely heart from Richard's hand:
He that perforce robs lions of their hearts

    May easily win a woman's.... Ay, my mother,
270 With all my heart I thank thee for my father!
    Who lives and dares but say thou didst not well
    When I was got, I'll send his soul to hell....
    Come, lady, I will show thee to my kin,
      And they shall say, when Richard me begot,
    If thou hadst said him nay, it had been sin:
      Who says it was, he lies; I say 'twas not.

                                      [they go

[2. 1.]   *France. Before Angiers*

*Enter KING PHILIP of France, LEWIS the Dauphin,
CONSTANCE and ARTHUR, meeting the DUKE OF AUSTRIA
(clad in a lion-skin) and his forces*

    K. Philip. Before Angiers well met, brave Austria.
Arthur, that great forerunner of thy blood,
Richard, that robbed the lion of his heart
And fought the holy wars in Palestine,
By this brave duke came early to his grave:
And for amends to his posterity,
At our importance hither is he come,
To spread his colours, boy, in thy behalf,
And to rebuke the usurpation
10 Of thy unnatural uncle, English John.
Embrace him, love him, give him welcome hither.
    Arthur. God shall forgive you Cordelion's death
The rather that you give his offspring life,
Shadowing their right under your wings of war:
I give you welcome with a powerless hand,
But with a heart full of unstainéd love.
Welcome before the gates of Angiers, duke.
    K. Philip. A noble boy! Who would not do thee right?

Austria. Upon thy cheek lay I this zealous kiss,
As seal to this indenture of my love: 20
That to my home I will no more return,
Till Angiers and the right thou hast in France,
Together with that pale, that white-faced shore,
Whose foot spurns back the ocean's roaring tides
And coops from other lands her islanders,
Even till that England, hedged in with the main,
That water-walléd bulwark, still secure
And confident from foreign purposes,
Even till that utmost corner of the west
Salute thee for her king—till then, fair boy,   30
Will I not think of home, but follow arms.
    Constance. O, take his mother's thanks, a
            widow's thanks,
Till your strong hand shall help to give him strength,
To make a more requital to your love.
    Austria. The peace of heaven is theirs that lift
            their swords
In such a just and charitable war.
    K. Philip. Well then, to work; our cannon shall
            be bent
Against the brows of this resisting town.
Call for our chiefest men of discipline,
To cull the plots of best advantages: 40
We'll lay before this town our royal bones,
Wade to the market-place in Frenchmen's blood,
But we will make it subject to this boy.
    Constance. Stay for an answer to your embassy,
Lest unadvised you stain your swords with blood.
My Lord Chatillion may from England bring
That right in peace which here we urge in war,
And then we shall repent each drop of blood
That hot rash haste so indirectly shed.

'Enter CHATILLION'

50   *K. Philip.* A wonder, lady! lo, upon thy wish,
Our messenger Chatillion is arrived.
What England says, say briefly, gentle lord,
We coldly pause for thee, Chatillion, speak.
    Chatillion. Then turn your forces from this
        paltry siege,
And stir them up against a mightier task:
England, impatient of your just demands,
Hath put himself in arms. The adverse winds,
Whose leisure I have stayed, have given him time
To land his legions all as soon as I:
60 His marches are expedient to this town,
His forces strong, his soldiers confident:
With him along is come the mother-queen,
An Até stirring him to blood and strife,
With her her niece, the Lady Blanch of Spain,
With them a bastard of the king's deceased,
And all th'unsettled humours of the land,
Rash, inconsiderate, fiery voluntaries,
With ladies' faces and fierce dragons' spleens,
Have sold their fortunes at their native homes,
70 Bearing their birthrights proudly on their backs,
To make a hazard of new fortunes here:
In brief, a braver choice of dauntless spirits
Than now the English bottoms have waft o'er
Did never float upon the swelling tide,
To do offence and scath in Christendom:
                        ['drum beats'
The interruption of their churlish drums
Cuts off more circumstance. They are at hand,
To parley or to fight, therefore prepare.
    K. Philip. How much unlooked for is this expedition!
80   *Austria.* By how much unexpected, by so much

We must awake endeavour for defence,
For courage mounteth with occasion.
Let them be welcome then, we are prepared.

Enter KING JOHN, ELINOR, BLANCH, the BASTARD,
PEMBROKE, and forces

K. John. Peace be to France: if France in peace
　　permit
Our just and lineal entrance to our own;
If not, bleed France, and peace ascend to heaven,
Whiles we, God's wrathful agent, do correct
Their proud contempt that beats his peace to heaven.
K. Philip. Peace be to England, if that war return
From France to England, there to live in peace:　　90
England we love, and for that England's sake
With burden of our armour here we sweat:
This toil of ours should be a work of thine;
But thou from loving England art so far,
That thou hast under-wrought his lawful king,
Cut off the sequence of posterity,
Out-facéd infant state, and done a rape
Upon the maiden virtue of the crown:
Look here upon thy brother Geffrey's face—
These eyes, these brows, were moulded out of his;　　100
This little abstract doth contain that large
Which died in Geffrey; and the hand of time
Shall draw this brief into as huge a volume:
That Geffrey was thy elder brother born,
And this his son: England was Geffrey's right,
　　　　　　　　　　[he points to Angiers
And this is Geffrey's in the name of God:
How comes it then that thou art called a king,
When living blood doth in these temples beat,
Which owe the crown that thou o'ermasterest?

　　　　　　　　　　　　　2-2

110   *K. John.* From whom hast thou this great
         commission, France,
  To draw my answer from thy articles?
    K. Philip. From that supernal judge, that stirs
        good thoughts
  In any breast of strong authority,
  To look into the blots and stains of right.
  That judge hath made me guardian to this boy,
  Under whose warrant I impeach thy wrong,
  And by whose help I mean to chastise it.
    K. John. Alack, thou dost usurp authority.
    K. Philip. Excuse it is, to beat usurping down.
120 *Elinor.* Who is it thou dost call usurper, France?
    Constance. Let me make answer: thy usurping son.
    Elinor. Out, insolent! thy bastard shall be king,
  That thou mayst be a queen, and check the world!
    Constance. My bed was ever to thy son as true,
  As thine was to thy husband, and this boy
  Liker in feature to his father Geffrey
  Than thou and John in manners; being as like
  As rain to water, or devil to his dam...
  My boy a bastard! By my soul, I think
130 His father never was so true begot—
  It cannot be an if thou wert his mother.
    Elinor. There's a good mother, boy, that blots
       thy father.
    Constance. There's a good grandam, boy, that would
       blot thee.
    Austria. Peace!
    Bastard.   Hear the crier.
    Austria.   What the devil art thou?
    Bastard. One that will play the devil, sir, with you,
  An a' may catch your hide and you alone:
  You are the hare of whom the proverb goes,

Whose valour plucks dead lions by the beard;
I'll smoke your skin-coat an I catch you right.
Sirrah, look to't, i'faith I will, i'faith.   140

  Blanch. O, well did he become that lion's robe
That did disrobe the lion of that robe!

  Bastard. It lies as sightly on the back of him,
As great Alcides' shows upon an ass:
But, ass, I'll take that burden from your back,
Or lay on that shall make your shoulders crack.

  Austria. What cracker is this same that deafs our ears
With this abundance of superfluous breath?
King Philip, determine what we shall do straight.

  K. Philip. Women and fools, break off   150
       your conference....
King John, this is the very sum of all:
England and Ireland, Anjou, Touraine, Maine,
In right of Arthur do I claim of thee:
Wilt thou resign them and lay down thy arms?

  K. John. My life as soon: I do defy thee, France.
Arthur of Britain, yield thee to my hand,
And out of my dear love I'll give thee more
Than e'er the coward hand of France can win:
Submit thee, boy.

  Elinor.   Come to thy grandam, child.

  Constance. Do, child, go to it grandam, child,   160
Give grandam kingdom, and it grandam will
Give it a plum, a cherry, and a fig.
There's a good grandam.

  Arthur.   Good my mother, peace!
I would that I were low laid in my grave,
I am not worth this coil that's made for me.

  Elinor. His mother shames him so, poor boy, he weeps.

  Constance. Now shame upon you, whe'r she does or no!
His grandam's wrongs, and not his mother's shames,

Draw those heaven-moving pearls from his poor eyes,
170 Which heaven shall take in nature of a fee:
Ay, with these crystal beads heaven shall be bribed
To do him justice and revenge on you.
    Elinor. Thou monstrous slanderer of heaven and earth!
    Constance. Thou monstrous injurer of heaven
        and earth!
Call not me slanderer; thou and thine usurp
The dominations, royalties and rights
Of this oppressèd boy: this is thy eldest son's son,
Infortunate in nothing but in thee:
Thy sins are visited in this poor child,
180 The canon of the law is laid on him,
Being but the second generation
Removèd from thy sin-conceiving womb.
    K. John. Bedlam, have done.
    Constance.   I have but this to say,
That he's not only plagued for her sin,
But God hath made her sin and her the plague
On this removèd issue, plagued for her
And with her plague, her sin; his injury
Her injury, the beadle to her sin—
All punished in the person of this child,
190 And all for her—a plague upon her!
    Elinor. Thou unadvisèd scold, I can produce
A will that bars the title of thy son.
    Constance. Ay, who doubts that? a will! a wicked will,
A woman's will, a cank'red grandam's will!
    K. Philip. Peace, lady! pause, or be more temperate.
It ill beseems this presence to cry aim
To these ill-tunèd repetitions:
Some trumpet summon hither to the walls
These men of Angiers—let us hear them speak
200 Whose title they admit, Arthur's or John's.

'*Trumpet sounds. Enter a Citizen upon the walls*'

Citizen. Who is it that hath warned us to the walls?
K. Philip. 'Tis France, for England.
K. John.   England, for itself:
You men of Angiers, and my loving subjects—
K. Philip. You loving men of Angiers,
    Arthur's subjects,
Our trumpet called you to this gentle parle.
K. John. For our advantage—therefore, hear us first:
These flags of France, that are advancéd here
Before the eye and prospect of your town,
Have hither marched to your endamagement:
The cannons have their bowels full of wrath,   210
And ready mounted are they to spit forth
Their iron indignation 'gainst your walls:
All preparation for a bloody siege
And merciless proceeding by these French
Confronts your city's eyes, your winking gates;
And but for our approach those sleeping stones,
That as a waist doth girdle you about,
By the compulsion of their ordinance
By this time from their fixéd beds of lime
Had been dishabited, and wide havoc made   220
For bloody power to rush upon your peace.
But on the sight of us your lawful king,
Who painfully with much expedient march
Have brought a countercheck before your gates,
To save unscratched your city's threat'ned cheeks,
Behold, the French amazed vouchsafe a parle:
And now, instead of bullets wrapped in fire,
To make a shaking fever in your walls,
They shoot but calm words folded up in smoke,
To make a faithless error in your ears: 230

Which trust accordingly, kind citizens,
And let us in, your king, whose laboured spirits,
Forwearied in this action of swift speed,
Crave harbourage within your city walls.
  K. Philip. When I have said, make answer to us both.
Lo, in this right hand, whose protection
Is most divinely vowed upon the right
Of him it holds, stands young Plantagenet,
Son to the elder brother of this man,
240 And king o'er him and all that he enjoys:
For this down-trodden equity, we tread
In warlike march these greens before your town,
Being no further enemy to you
Than the constraint of hospitable zeal
In the relief of this oppressèd child
Religiously provokes. Be pleasèd then
To pay that duty which you truly owe
To him that owes it, namely this young prince,
And then our arms, like to a muzzled bear,
250 Save in aspect, hath all offence sealed up:
Our cannons' malice vainly shall be spent
Against th'invulnerable clouds of heaven,
And with a blessèd and unvexed retire,
With unhacked swords and helmets all unbruised,
We will bear home that lusty blood again
Which here we came to spout against your town,
And leave your children, wives, and you in peace....
But if you fondly pass our proffered offer,
'Tis not the roundure of your old-faced walls
260 Can hide you from our messengers of war,
Though all these English and their discipline
Were harboured in their rude circumference:
Then tell us, shall your city call us lord,
In that behalf which we have challenged it?

Or shall we give the signal to our rage
And stalk in blood to our possession?
  Citizen. In brief, we are the King of
      England's subjects:
For him, and in his right, we hold this town.
  K. John. Acknowledge then the king, and let me in.
  Citizen. That can we not: but he that proves the king, 270
To him will we prove loyal. Till that time
Have we rammed up our gates against the world.
  K. John. Doth not the crown of England prove
      the king?
And, if not that, I bring you witnesses,
Twice fifteen thousand hearts of England's breed—
  Bastard. Bastards and else.
  K. John. To verify our title with their lives.
  K. Philip. As many and as well-born bloods as those—
  Bastard. Some bastards too.
  K. Philip. Stand in his face to contradict his claim.   280
  Citizen. Till you compound whose right is worthiest,
We for the worthiest hold the right from both.
  K. John. Then God forgive the sin of all those souls
That to their everlasting residence,
Before the dew of evening fall, shall fleet,
In dreadful trial of our kingdom's king!
  K. Philip. Amen, amen! Mount, chevaliers! to arms!
  Bastard. Saint George, that swinged the dragon, and
      e'er since
Sits on his horse back at mine hostess' door,
Teach us some fence! [*to Austria*] Sirrah, were I at home, 290
At your den, sirrah, with your lioness,
I would set an ox-head to your lion's hide,
And make a monster of you.
  Austria.   Peace, no more.
  Bastard. O, tremble! for you hear the lion roar.

K. John. Up higher to the plain, where we'll set forth
In best appointment all our regiments.
    Bastard. Speed then to take advantage of the field.
    K. Philip. It shall be so, and at the other hill
Command the rest to stand. God, and our right!

                                           [they go

     '*Here, after excursions, enter the Herald of France*
                with Trumpets to the gates'

300   *French Herald.* You men of Angiers, open wide
        your gates,
And let young Arthur, Duke of Britain, in,
Who by the hand of France this day hath made
Much work for tears in many an English mother,
Whose sons lie scattered on the bleeding ground:
Many a widow's husband grovelling lies,
Coldly embracing the discoloured earth,
And victory with little loss doth play
Upon the dancing banners of the French,
Who are at hand, triumphantly displayed,
310 To enter conquerors, and to proclaim
Arthur of Britain England's king and yours.

       '*Enter English Herald with Trumpet*'

    English. Herald. Rejoice, you men of Angiers, ring
        your bells,
King John, your king and England's, doth approach,
Commander of this hot malicious day!
Their armours, that marched hence so silver-bright,
Hither return all gilt with Frenchmen's blood:
There stuck no plume in any English crest,
That is removéd by a staff of France:
Our colours do return in those same hands
320 That did display them when we first marched forth;

And like a jolly troop of huntsmen come
Our lusty English, all with purpled hands,
Dyed in the dying slaughter of their foes.
Open your gates and give the victors way.
　Citizen.　Heralds, from off our towers we
　　　　might behold,
From first to last, the onset and retire
Of both your armies, whose equality
By our best eyes cannot be censuréd:
Blood hath bought blood, and blows have
　　　　answered blows;
Strength matched with strength, and power
　　　　confronted power.　　　　　　　　330
Both are alike, and both alike we like:
One must prove greatest: while they weigh so even,
We hold our town for neither; yet for both.

　'Enter the two KINGS with their powers' severally

　K. John.　France, hast thou yet more blood to
　　　　cast away?
Say, shall the current of our right run on?
Whose passage, vexed with thy impediment,
Shall leave his native channel, and o'erswell
With course disturbed even thy confining shores,
Unless thou let his silver water keep
A peaceful progress to the ocean.　　　　340
　K. Philip.　England, thou hast not saved one drop
　　　　of blood
In this hot trial more than we of France,
Rather lost more. And by this hand I swear,
That sways the earth this climate overlooks,
Before we will lay down our just-borne arms,
We'll put thee down, 'gainst whom these arms we bear,
Or add a royal number to the dead,

Gracing the scroll that tells of this war's loss
With slaughter coupled to the name of kings.

350 *Bastard.* Ha, majesty! how high thy glory towers,
When the rich blood of kings is set on fire!
O, now doth death line his dead chaps with steel,
The swords of soldiers are his teeth, his fangs,
And now he feasts, mousing the flesh of men,
In undetermined differences of kings....
Why stand these royal fronts amazéd thus?
Cry 'havoc!' kings, back to the stainéd field,
You equal potents, fiery-kindled spirits!
Then let confusion of one part confirm
360 The other's peace; till then, blows, blood, and death!

    K. John. Whose party do the townsmen yet admit?

    K. Philip. Speak, citizens, for England; who's
        your king?

    Citizen. The King of England, when we know
        the king.

    K. Philip. Know him in us, that here hold up
        his right.

    K. John. In us, that are our own great deputy,
And bear possession of our person here,
Lord of our presence, Angiers, and of you.

    Citizen. A greater power than we denies all this,
And till it be undoubted, we do lock
370 Our former scruple in our strong-barred gates:
Kinged of our fears, until our fears, resolved,
Be by some certain king purged and deposed.

    Bastard. By heaven, these scroyles of Angiers flout
        you, kings,
And stand securely on their battlements,
As in a theatre, whence they gape and point
At your industrious scenes and acts of death.
Your royal presences be ruled by me,
Do like the mutines of Jerusalem

Be friends awhile and both conjointly bend
Your sharpest deeds of malice on this town: 380
By east and west let France and England mount
Their battering cannon chargéd to the mouths,
Till their soul-fearing clamours have brawled down
The flinty ribs of this contemptuous city.
I'ld play incessantly upon these jades,
Even till unfencéd desolation
Leave them as naked as the vulgar air:
That done, dissever your united strengths,
And part your mingled colours once again,
Turn face to face, and bloody point to point: 390
Then in a moment Fortune shall cull forth
Out of one side her happy minion,
To whom in favour she shall give the day,
And kiss him with a glorious victory...
How like you this wild counsel, mighty states?
Smacks it not something of the policy?

    K. John.   Now, by the sky that hangs above our heads,
I like it well. France, shall we knit our powers
And lay this Angiers even with the ground,
Then after fight who shall be king of it?   400

    Bastard.   An if thou hast the mettle of a king,
Being wronged as we are by this peevish town,
Turn thou the mouth of thy artillery,
As we will ours, against these saucy walls,
And when that we have dashed them to the ground,
Why then defy each other, and pell-mell
Make work upon ourselves, for heaven or hell.

    K. Philip.   Let it be so: say, where will you assault?

    K. John.   We from the west will send destruction
Into this city's bosom.   410

    Austria.   I from the north.

    K. Philip.   Our thunder from the south,
Shall rain their drift of bullets on this town.

(Bastard. O prudent discipline! From north to south:
Austria and France shoot in each other's mouth.
I'll stir them to it...[*shouts*] Come, away, away!
    Citizen. Hear us, great kings, vouchsafe awhile to stay
And I shall show you peace and fair-faced league:
Win you this city without stroke or wound,
Rescue those breathing lives to die in beds,
420 That here come sacrifices for the field:
Persever not, but hear me, mighty kings.
    K. John. Speak on with favour, we are bent to hear.
    Citizen. That daughter there of Spain, the
            Lady Blanch,
Is niece to England. Look upon the years
Of Lewis the Dauphin and that lovely maid:
If lusty love should go in quest of beauty,
Where should he find it fairer than in Blanch?
If zealous love should go in search of virtue,
Where should he find it purer than in Blanch?
430 If love ambitious sought a match of birth,
Whose veins bound richer blood than Lady Blanch?
Such as she is, in beauty, virtue, birth,
Is the young Dauphin every way complete:
†If not complete of, say he is not she,
And she again wants nothing, to name want,
If want it be not that she is not he:
He is the half part of a blessèd man,
Left to be finishèd by such a she;
And she a fair divided excellence,
440 Whose fulness of perfection lies in him.
O, two such silver currents when they join
Do glorify the banks that bound them in:
And two such shores to two such streams made one,
Two such controlling bounds shall you be, kings,
To these two princes, if you marry them:

This union shall do more than battery can
To our fast-closéd gates; for at this match,
With swifter spleen than powder can enforce,
The mouth of passage shall we fling wide ope,
And give you entrance; but, without this match,   450
The sea enragéd is not half so deaf,
Lions more confident, mountains and rocks
More free from motion, no, not Death himself
In mortal fury half so peremptory,
As we to keep this city.

 Bastard.   Here's a stay
That shakes the rotten carcass of old Death
Out of his rags! Here's a large mouth, indeed,
That spits forth death and mountains, rocks and seas,
Talks as familiarly of roaring lions
As maids of thirteen do of puppy-dogs!   460
What cannoneer begot this lusty blood?
He speaks plain cannon fire, and smoke and bounce,
He gives the bastinado with his tongue:
Our ears are cudgelled—not a word of his
But buffets better than a fist of France:
Zounds! I was never so bethumped with words
Since I first called my brother's father 'dad'.

 (*Elinor.* Son, list to this conjunction, make this match;
Give with our niece a dowry large enough,
For by this knot thou shalt so surely tie   470
Thy now unsured assurance to the crown,
That yon green boy shall have no sun to ripe
The bloom that promiseth a mighty fruit.
I see a yielding in the looks of France:
Mark how they whisper, urge them while their souls
Are capable of this ambition,
Lest zeal, now melted by the windy breath
Of soft petitions, pity and remorse,

Cool and congeal again to what it was.

480 *Citizen.* Why answer not the double majesties
This friendly treaty of our threat'ned town?

    K. Philip. Speak England first, that hath been
      forward first
To speak unto this city: what say you?

    K. John. If that the Dauphin there, thy princely son,
Can in this book of beauty read 'I love',
Her dowry shall weigh equal with a queen:
For Anjou, and fair Touraine, Maine, Poictiers,
And all that we upon this side the sea
(Except this city now by us besieged)
490 Find liable to our crown and dignity,
Shall gild her bridal bed, and make her rich
In titles, honours and promotions,
As she in beauty, education, blood,
Holds hand with any princess of the world.

    K. Philip. What say'st thou, boy? look in the
      lady's face.

    Lewis. I do, my lord, and in her eye I find
A wonder, or a wondrous miracle,
The shadow of myself formed in her eye,
Which, being but the shadow of your son,
500 Becomes a sun, and makes your son a shadow:
I do protest, I never loved myself,
Till now infixéd I beheld myself,
Drawn in the flattering table of her eye.
                  ['*whispers with Blanch*'
  (*Bastard.* Drawn in the flattering table of her eye,
    Hanged in the frowning wrinkle of her brow,
And quartered in her heart, he doth espy
    Himself love's traitor. This is pity now:
That hanged, and drawn, and quartered, there should be
In such a love so vile a lout as he.

Blanch. [*to Lewis*] My uncle's will in this respect   510
    is mine.
If he see aught in you that makes him like,
That anything he sees, which moves his liking,
I can with ease translate it to my will:
Or if you will, to speak more properly,
I will enforce it easily to my love.
Further I will not flatter you, my lord,
That all I see in you is worthy love,
Than this—that nothing do I see in you,
Though churlish thoughts themselves should be
        your judge,
That I can find should merit any hate.   520
    K. John. What say these young ones? What say you,
        my niece?
Blanch. That she is bound in honour still to do
What you in wisdom still vouchsafe to say.
    K. John. Speak then, Prince Dauphin, can you love
        this lady?
Lewis. Nay, ask me if I can refrain from love,
For I do love her most unfeignedly.
    K. John. Then do I give Volquessen,
        Touraine, Maine,
Poictiers and Anjou, these five provinces,
With her to thee, and this addition more,
Full thirty thousand marks of English coin: 530
Philip of France, if thou be pleased withal,
Command thy son and daughter to join hands.
    K. Philip. It likes us well; young princes, close
        your hands.
Austria. And your lips too, for I am well assured
That I did so when I was first assured.
    K. Philip. Now, citizens of Angiers, ope your gates,
Let in that amity which you have made,

For at Saint Mary's chapel presently
The rites of marriage shall be solemnized.
540 Is not the Lady Constance in this troop?
I know she is not, for this match made up
Her presence would have interrupted much:
Where is she and her son? tell me, who knows.

    Lewis. She is sad and passionate at your highness' tent.

    K. Philip. And, by my faith, this league that we
        have made
Will give her sadness very little cure:
Brother of England, how may we content
This widow lady? In her right we came,
Which we, God knows, have turned another way,
550 To our own vantage.

    K. John.   We will heal up all,
For we'll create young Arthur Duke of Britain
And Earl of Richmond, and this rich fair town
We make him lord of.…Call the Lady Constance.
Some speedy messenger bid her repair
To our solemnity: I trust we shall,
If not fill up the measure of her will,
Yet in some measure satisfy her so
That we shall stop her exclamation.
Go we, as well as haste will suffer us,
560 To this unlooked for, unpreparéd pomp.

              [they pass through the gates, leaving the
                       Bastard alone without

    Bastard. Mad world! mad kings! mad composition!
John, to stop Arthur's title in the whole,
Hath willingly departed with a part,
And France—whose armour conscience buckled on,
Whom zeal and charity brought to the field
As God's own soldier—rounded in the ear
With that same purpose-changer, that sly devil,

That broker that still breaks the pate of faith,
That daily break-vow, he that wins of all,
Of kings, of beggars, old men, young men, maids,   570
Who, having no external thing to lose
But the word 'maid', cheats the poor maid of that,
That smooth-faced gentleman, tickling Commodity,
Commodity, the bias of the world,
The world, who of itself is peiséd well,
Made to run even upon even ground,
Till this advantage, this vile-drawing bias,
This sway of motion, this Commodity,
Makes it take head from all indifferency,
From all direction, purpose, course, intent: 580
And this same bias, this Commodity,
This bawd, this broker, this all-changing word,
Clapped on the outward eye of fickle France,
Hath drawn him from his own determined aid,
From a resolved and honourable war,
To a most base and vile-concluded peace....
And why rail I on this Commodity?
But for because he hath not wooed me yet:
Not that I have the power to clutch my hand,
When his fair angels would salute my palm,   590
But for my hand, as unattempted yet,
Like a poor beggar, raileth on the rich:
Well, whiles I am a beggar, I will rail,
And say there is no sin but to be rich;
And being rich, my virtue then shall be
To say there is no vice but beggary:
Since kings break faith upon commodity,
Gain, be my lord, for I will worship thee.   [*he goes in*

3-2

[3. 1.]   *Without the French KING's tent;*
             a grassy knoll near-by

'*Enter* CONSTANCE, ARTHUR, *and* SALISBURY'

Constance. Gone to be married! gone to swear a peace!
False blood to false blood joined! gone to be friends!
Shall Lewis have Blanch, and Blanch those provinces?
It is not so, thou hast misspoke, misheard,
Be well advised, tell o'er thy tale again.
It cannot be, thou dost but say 'tis so.
I trust I may not trust thee, for thy word
Is but the vain breath of a common man:
Believe me, I do not believe thee, man,
10 I have a king's oath to the contrary.
Thou shalt be punished for thus frighting me,
For I am sick and capable of fears,
Oppressed with wrongs, and therefore full of fears,
A widow, husbandless, subject to fears,
A woman naturally born to fears;
And though thou now confess thou didst but jest,
With my vexed spirits I cannot take a truce,
But they will quake and tremble all this day....
What dost thou mean by shaking of thy head?
20 Why dost thou look so sadly on my son?
What means that hand upon that breast of thine?
Why holds thine eye that lamentable rheum,
Like a proud river peering o'er his bounds?
Be these sad signs confirmers of thy words?
Then speak again, not all thy former tale,
But this one word, whether thy tale be true.
Salisbury. As true as I believe you think them false
That give you cause to prove my saying true.

Constance. O, if thou teach me to believe this sorrow,
Teach thou this sorrow how to make me die,   30
And let belief and life encounter so
As doth the fury of two desperate men
Which in the very meeting fall and die....
Lewis marry Blanch! O boy, then where art thou?
France friend with England, what becomes of me?
Fellow, be gone: I cannot brook thy sight—
This news hath made thee a most ugly man.
  Salisbury. What other harm have I, good lady, done,
But spoke the harm that is by others done?
  Constance. Which harm within itself so heinous is   40
As it makes harmful all that speak of it.
  Arthur. I do beseech you, madam, be content.
  Constance. If thou, that bid'st me be content, wert grim,
Ugly and sland'rous to thy mother's womb,
Full of unpleasing blots and sightless stains,
Lame, foolish, crooked, swart, prodigious,
Patched with foul moles and eye-offending marks,
I would not care, I then would be content,
For then I should not love thee; no, nor thou
Become thy great birth nor deserve a crown.   50
But thou art fair, and at thy birth, dear boy,
Nature and Fortune joined to make thee great.
Of Nature's gifts thou mayst with lilies boast
And with the half-blown rose. But Fortune, O,
She is corrupted, changed and won from thee;
Sh'adulterates hourly with thine uncle John,
And with her golden hand hath plucked on France
To tread down fair respect of sovereignty,
And made his majesty the bawd to theirs.
France is a bawd to Fortune and King John,   60
That strumpet Fortune, that usurping John:
Tell me, thou fellow, is not France forsworn?

Envenom him with words, or get thee gone,
And leave those woes alone which I alone
Am bound to under-bear.

    Salisbury.   Pardon me, madam,
I may not go without you to the kings.

    Constance. Thou mayst, thou shalt, I will not go
        with thee.

                  [*she turns from him and ascends the knoll*
I will instruct my sorrows to be proud,
For grief is proud and makes his owner stoop.
70 To me and to the state of my great grief
Let kings assemble; for my grief's so great
That no supporter but the huge firm earth
Can hold it up: here I and sorrows sit,
Here is my throne, bid kings come bow to it.

                  [*she seats herself on the knoll*

  Enter KING JOHN, KING PHILIP, LEWIS, BLANCH,
    ELINOR, *the* BASTARD, AUSTRIA, *and attendants*

    K. Philip. 'Tis true, fair daughter, and this blessed day
Ever in France shall be kept festival:
To solemnize this day, the glorious sun
Stays in his course and plays the alchemist,
Turning with splendour of his precious eye
80 The meagre cloddy earth to glittering gold:
The yearly course that brings this day about
Shall never see it but a holiday.

    Constance. [*from above*] A wicked day, and not a
        holy day!
What hath this day deserved? what hath it done,
That it in golden letters should be set
Among the high tides in the calendar?
Nay, rather turn this day out of the week,
This day of shame, oppression, perjury.
Or, if it must stand still, let wives with child

Pray that their burdens may not fall this day,   90
Lest that their hopes prodigiously be crossed:
But on this day let seamen fear no wrack,
No bargains break that are not this day made:
This day, all things begun come to ill end;
Yea, faith itself to hollow falsehood change!
  K. Philip. By heaven, lady, you shall have no cause
To curse the fair proceedings of this day:
Have I not pawned to you my majesty?
  Constance. You have beguiled me with a counterfeit
Resembling majesty, which being touched and tried   100
Proves valueless: you are forsworn, forsworn!
You came in arms to spill mine enemies' blood,
But now in arms you strengthen it with yours.
The grappling vigour and rough frown of war
Is cold in amity and painted peace,
And our oppression hath made up this league...
Arm, arm, you heavens, against these perjured kings!
A widow cries; be husband to me, heavens!
Let not the hours of this ungodly day
Wear out the day in peace; but, ere sun set,   110
Set arméd discord 'twixt these perjured kings!
Hear me, O, hear me!
  Austria.   Lady Constance, peace.
  Constance. War! war! no peace! peace is to me a war:
O Lymoges! O Austria! thou dost shame
That bloody spoil: thou slave, thou wretch, thou coward,
Thou little valiant, great in villany!
Thou ever strong upon the stronger side!
Thou Fortune's champion, that dost never fight
But when her humorous ladyship is by
To teach thee safety! thou art perjured too,   120
And sooth'st up greatness. What a fool art thou,
A ramping fool, to brag and stamp and swear
Upon my party! Thou cold-blooded slave,

Hast thou not spoke like thunder on my side,
Been sworn my soldier, bidding me depend
Upon thy stars, thy fortune and thy strength,
And dost thou now fall over to my foes?
Thou wear a lion's hide! doff it for shame,
And hang a calf's-skin on those recreant limbs.

130 *Austria.* O, that a man should speak those words to me!
Bastard. And hang a calf's-skin on those recreant limbs.
Austria. Thou dar'st not say so, villain, for thy life.
Bastard. And hang a calf's-skin on those recreant limbs.
K. John. We like not this, thou dost forget thyself.

'*Enter PANDULPH*'

K. Philip. Here comes the holy legate of the Pope.
Pandulph. Hail, you anointed deputies of heaven!
To thee, King John, my holy errand is:
I Pandulph, of fair Milan cardinal,
And from Pope Innocent the legate here,

140 Do in his name religiously demand
Why thou against the church, our holy mother,
So wilfully dost spurn; and force perforce
Keep Stephen Langton, chosen archbishop
Of Canterbury, from that holy see:
This, in our foresaid holy father's name,
Pope Innocent, I do demand of thee.

K. John. What earthly name to interrogatories
Can task the free breath of a sacred king?
Thou canst not, cardinal, devise a name

150 So slight, unworthy and ridiculous,
To charge me to an answer, as the Pope:
Tell him this tale, and from the mouth of England
Add thus much more, that no Italian priest
Shall tithe or toll in our dominions;
But as we, under heaven, are supreme head,

So under Him that great supremacy,
Where we do reign, we will alone uphold,
Without th' assistance of a mortal hand:
So tell the Pope, all reverence set apart
To him and his usurped authority.   160
  K. Philip. Brother of England, you blaspheme in this.
  K. John. Though you and all the kings of
      Christendom
Are led so grossly by this meddling priest,
Dreading the curse that money may buy out,
And by the merit of vile gold, dross, dust,
Purchase corrupted pardon of a man,
Who in that sale sells pardon from himself;
Though you and all the rest so grossly led
This juggling witchcraft with revenue cherish,
Yet I alone, alone do me oppose   170
Against the Pope and count his friends my foes.
  Pandulph. Then, by the lawful power that I have,
Thou shalt stand cursed and excommunicate,
And blessèd shall he be that doth revolt
From his allegiance to an heretic,
And meritorious shall that hand be called,
Canónizèd and worshipped as a saint,
That takes away by any secret course
Thy hateful life.
  Constance.   O, lawful let it be
That I have room with Rome to curse awhile!   180
Good father cardinal, cry thou amen
To my keen curses; for without my wrong
There is no tongue hath power to curse him right.
  Pandulph. There's law and warrant, lady, for my curse.
  Constance. And for mine too. When law can do no right,
Let it be lawful that law bar no wrong:
Law cannot give my child his kingdom here;

For he that holds his kingdom holds the law:
Therefore, since law itself is perfect wrong,
190 How can the law forbid my tongue to curse?
    Pandulph. Philip of France, on peril of a curse,
Let go the hand of that arch-heretic,
And raise the power of France upon his head,
Unless he do submit himself to Rome.
    Elinor. Look'st thou pale, France? do not let go
      thy hand.
    Constance. Look to that, devil, lest that France repent,
And by disjoining hands, hell lose a soul.
    Austria. King Philip, listen to the cardinal.
    Bastard. And hang a calf's-skin on his recreant limbs.
200 *Austria.* Well, ruffian, I must pocket up these wrongs,
Because—
    Bastard. Your breeches best may carry them.
    K. John. Philip, what say'st thou to the cardinal?
    Constance. What should he say, but as the cardinal?
    Lewis. Bethink you, father, for the difference
Is purchase of a heavy curse from Rome,
Or the light loss of England for a friend:
Forgo the easier.
    Blanch.   That's the curse of Rome.
    Constance. O Lewis, stand fast, the devil tempts thee here
In likeness of a new untrimméd bride.
210 *Blanch.* The Lady Constance speaks not from her faith,
But from her need.
    Constance.   O, if thou grant my need,
Which only lives but by the death of faith,
That need must needs infer this principle,
That faith would live again by death of need:
O then, tread down my need, and faith mounts up,
Keep my need up, and faith is trodden down.
    K. John. The king is moved, and answers not to this.
    Constance. O, be removed from him, and answer well.

Austria. Do so, King Philip, hang no more in doubt.
Bastard. Hang nothing but a calf's-skin, most sweet lout. 220
K. Philip. I am perplexed, and know not what to say.
Pandulph. What canst thou say but will perplex
    thee more,
If thou stand excommunicate and cursed?
    K. Philip. Good reverend father, make my
       person yours,
And tell me how you would bestow yourself.
This royal hand and mine are newly knit,
And the conjunction of our inward souls
Married in league, coupled and linked together
With all religious strength of sacred vows:
The latest breath that gave the sound of words   230
Was deep-sworn faith, peace, amity, true love
Between our kingdoms and our royal selves,
And even before this truce, but new before,
No longer than we well could wash our hands
To clap this royal bargain up of peace,
Heaven knows, they were besmeared and overstained
With slaughter's pencil, where revenge did paint
The fearful difference of incensèd kings:
And shall these hands, so lately purged of blood,
So newly joined in love, so strong in both,   240
Unyoke this seizure and this kind regreet?
Play fast and loose with faith? so jest with heaven,
Make such unconstant children of ourselves,
As now again to snatch our palm from palm,
Unswear faith sworn, and on the marriage-bed
Of smiling peace to march a bloody host,
And make a riot on the gentle brow
Of true sincerity? O holy sir,
My reverend father, let it not be so:
Out of your grace, devise, ordain, impose   250
Some gentle order, and then we shall be blest

To do your pleasure and continue friends.
   Pandulph. All form is formless, order orderless,
Save what is opposite to England's love.
Therefore, to arms! be champion of our church,
Or let the church, our mother, breathe her curse,
A mother's curse, on her revolting son:
France, thou mayst hold a serpent by the tongue,
A chaféd lion by the mortal paw,
260 A fasting tiger safer by the tooth,
Than keep in peace that hand which thou dost hold.
   K. Philip. I may disjoin my hand, but not my faith.
   Pandulph. So mak'st thou faith an enemy to faith,
And like a civil war set'st oath to oath,
Thy tongue against thy tongue. O, let thy vow
First made to heaven, first be to heaven performed,
That is, to be the champion of our church.
What since thou swor'st is sworn against thyself
And may not be perforḿed by thyself,
270 For that which thou hast sworn to do amiss
Is not amiss when it is truly done;
And being not done, where doing tends to ill,
The truth is then most done not doing it:
The better act of purposes mistook
Is to mistake again; though indirect,
Yet indirection thereby grows direct,
And falsehood falsehood cures, as fire cools fire
Within the scorchéd veins of one new-burned:
It is religion that doth make vows kept,
280 But thou hast sworn against religion,
By what thou swear'st against the thing thou swear'st,
And mak'st an oath the surety for thy truth
Against an oath: the truth thou art unsure
To swear, swears only not to be forsworn;
Else what a mockery should it be to swear!

But thou dost swear only to be forsworn,
And most forsworn to keep what thou dost swear.
Therefore thy later vows against thy first
Is in thyself rebellion to thyself:
And better conquest never canst thou make   290
Than arm thy constant and thy nobler parts
Against these giddy loose suggestions:
Upon which better part our prayers come in,
If thou vouchsafe them: but if not, then know
The peril of our curses light on thee
So heavy as thou shalt not shake them off,
But in despair die under their black weight.
   Austria. Rebellion, flat rebellion!
   Bastard.   Will't not be?
Will not a calf's-skin stop that mouth of thine?
   Lewis. Father, to arms!
   Blanch.   Upon thy wedding-day?   300
Against the blood that thou hast marriéd?
What, shall our feast be kept with slaughtered men?
Shall braying trumpets and loud churlish drums,
Clamours of hell, be measures to our pomp?
O husband, hear me! ay, alack, how new
Is husband in my mouth! even for that name,
Which till this time my tongue did ne'er pronounce,
Upon my knee I beg, go not to arms
Against mine uncle.
   Constance. [*descends and kneels*]   O, upon my knee,
Made hard with kneeling, I do pray to thee,   310
Thou virtuous Dauphin, alter not the doom
Forethought by heaven.
   Blanch. Now shall I see thy love. What motive may
Be stronger with thee than the name of wife?
   Constance. That which upholdeth him that
      thee upholds,

His honour. O, thine honour, Lewis, thine honour!

Lewis. I muse your majesty doth seem so cold,

When such profound respects do pull you on.

Pandulph. I will denounce a curse upon his head.

320 *K. Philip.* Thou shalt not need. England, I will fall from thee.

Constance. O fair return of banished majesty!

Elinor. O foul revolt of French inconstancy!

K. John. France, thou shalt rue this hour within this hour.

Bastard. Old Time the clock-setter, that bald sexton Time,

Is it as he will? well then, France shall rue.

Blanch. The sun's o'ercast with blood: fair day, adieu!

Which is the side that I must go withal?

I am with both. Each army hath a hand,

And in their rage, I having hold of both,

330 They whirl asunder and dismember me.

Husband, I cannot pray that thou mayst win;

Uncle, I needs must pray that thou mayst lose;

Father, I may not wish the fortune thine;

Grandam, I will not wish thy wishes thrive:

Whoever wins, on that side shall I lose;

Assuréd loss before the match be played.

Lewis. Lady, with me, with me thy fortune lies.

Blanch. There where my fortune lives, there my life dies.

K. John. Cousin, go draw our puissance together.

[*the Bastard hurries forth*

340 France, I am burned up with inflaming wrath,

A rage whose heat hath this condition,

That nothing can allay, nothing but blood,

The blood, and dearest-valued blood, of France.

K. Philip. Thy rage shall burn thee up, and thou shalt turn

To ashes, ere our blood shall quench that fire:
Look to thyself, thou art in jeopardy.

    K. John. No more than he that threats. To arms
        let's hie!   *[they go*

[3. 2.]   *Before Angiers*

      The battle begins. 'Alarums, excursions:
      enter the BASTARD, with AUSTRIA'S head'

Bastard. Now, by my life, this day grows
        wondrous hot,
Some airy devil hovers in the sky,
And pours down mischief. Austria's head lie there,
While Philip breathes.

    'Enter KING JOHN, ARTHUR, and HUBERT'

    K. John. Hubert, keep this boy...Philip, make up.
My mother is assailéd in our tent,
And ta'en, I fear.

    Bastard.   My lord, I rescued her,
Her highness is in safety, fear you not:
But on, my liege, for very little pains
Will bring this labour to an happy end.   *[they go* 10

[3. 3.] *After further alarums and excursions a retreat is
sounded, and KING JOHN enters in triumph with ELINOR,
ARTHUR, the BASTARD, HUBERT, and Lords*

    K. John [*to Elinor*]. So shall it be; your grace shall
        stay behind,
†More strongly guarded...[*to Arthur*] Cousin, look
        not sad.
Thy grandam loves thee, and thy uncle will
As dear be to thee as thy father was.

Arthur. O, this will make my mother die with grief.

K. John [to the Bastard]. Cousin, away for England!
    haste before,

And ere our coming see thou shake the bags

Of hoarding abbots; imprisoned angels

Set at liberty: the fat ribs of peace

10 Must by the hungry now be fed upon:

Use our commission in his utmost force.

    Bastard. Bell, book, and candle shall not drive
        me back,

When gold and silver becks me to come on.

I leave your highness: Grandam, I will pray

(If ever I remember to be holy)

For your fair safety; so I kiss your hand.

    Elinor. Farewell, gentle cousin.

    K. John.   Coz, farewell.   *[the Bastard goes*

    Elinor. Come hither, little kinsman; hark, a word.

    K. John. Come hither, Hubert. O my gentle Hubert,

20 We owe thee much; within this wall of flesh

There is a soul counts thee her creditor,

And with advantage means to pay thy love:

And, my good friend, thy voluntary oath

Lives in this bosom, dearly cherishéd....

Give me thy hand. I had a thing to say,

But I will fit it with some better time....

By heaven, Hubert, I am almost ashamed

To say what good respect I have of thee.

    Hubert. I am much bounden to your majesty.

30   *K. John.* Good friend, thou hast no cause to say
        so yet,

But thou shalt have; and creep time ne'er so slow,

Yet it shall come for me to do thee good....

I had a thing to say, but let it go:

The sun is in the heaven, and the proud day,

Attended with the pleasures of the world,
Is all too wanton and too full of gawds
To give me audience: if the midnight bell
Did, with his iron tongue and brazen mouth,
Sound on into the drowsy ear of night;
If this same were a churchyard where we stand,   40
And thou possesséd with a thousand wrongs;
Or if that surly spirit, melancholy,
Had baked thy blood and made it heavy-thick,
Which else runs tickling up and down the veins,
Making that idiot, laughter, keep men's eyes
And strain their cheeks to idle merriment,
A passion hateful to my purposes;
Or if that thou couldst see me without eyes,
Hear me without thine ears, and make reply
Without a tongue, using conceit alone,   50
Without eyes, ears and harmful sound of words;
†Then, in despite of broad-eyed watchful day,
I would into thy bosom pour my thoughts:
But, ah, I will not! yet I love thee well,
And, by my troth, I think, thou lov'st me well.
    Hubert. So well, that what you bid me undertake,
Though that my death were adjunct to my act,
By heaven, I would do it.
    K. John.   Do not I know thou wouldst?
Good Hubert, Hubert, Hubert, throw thine eye
On yon young boy: I'll tell thee what, my friend,   60
He is a very serpent in my way,
And wheresoe'er this foot of mine doth tread,
He lies before me: dost thou understand me?
Thou art his keeper.
    Hubert.   And I'll keep him so,
That he shall not offend your majesty.
    K. John.   Death.

4   P S K J

Hubert. My lord?

K. John.   A grave.

Hubert.   He shall not live.

K. John.   Enough....

I could be merry now. Hubert, I love thee.

Well, I'll not say what I intend for thee:

Remember...Madam, fare you well,

70 I'll send those powers o'er to your majesty.

   Elinor. My blessing go with thee!

   K. John.   For England, cousin, go.

Hubert shall be your man, attend on you

With all true duty...On toward Calais, ho!   [*they go*

[3. 4.]   *Before the French King's tent*

KING PHILIP, LEWIS, PANDULPH, *and attendants*

   K. Philip. So, by a roaring tempest on the flood,

A whole armado of convicted sail

Is scattered and disjoined from fellowship.

   Pandulph. Courage and comfort! all shall yet go well.

   K. Philip. What can go well, when we have run so ill?

Are we not beaten? Is not Angiers lost?

Arthur ta'en prisoner? divers dear friends slain?

And bloody England into England gone,

O'erbearing interruption, spite of France?

10 *Lewis.* What he hath won, that hath he fortified:

So hot a speed with such advice disposed,

Such temperate order in so fierce a cause,

Doth want example: who hath read or heard

Of any kindred action like to this?

   K. Philip. Well could I bear that England had
        this praise,

So we could find some pattern of our shame.

CONSTANCE enters, her hair loose about her shoulders

Look, who comes here! a grave unto a soul,
Holding th'eternal spirit, against her will,
In the vile prison of afflicted breath...
I prithee, lady, go away with me.   20
  Constance. Lo, now! now see the issue of your peace!
  K. Philip. Patience, good lady! comfort, gentle
      Constance!
  Constance. No, I defy all counsel, all redress,
But that which ends all counsel, true redress...
Death, death. O amiable lovely death!
Thou odoriferous stench! sound rottenness!
Arise forth from the couch of lasting night,
Thou hate and terror to prosperity,
And I will kiss thy detestable bones,
And put my eyeballs in thy vaulty brows,   30
And ring these fingers with thy household worms,
And stop this gap of breath with fulsome dust,
And be a carrion monster like thyself;
Come, grin on me, and I will think thou smil'st,
And buss thee as thy wife! Misery's love,
O, come to me!
  K. Philip.   O fair affliction, peace.
  Constance. No, no, I will not, having breath to cry:
O, that my tongue were in the thunder's mouth!
Then with a passion would I shake the world,
And rouse from sleep that fell anatomy,   40
Which cannot hear a lady's feeble voice,
Which scorns a modern invocation.
  Pandulph. Lady, you utter madness, and not sorrow.
  Constance. Thou art not holy to belie me so.
I am not mad: this hair I tear is mine,
My name is Constance, I was Geffrey's wife,

4-2

Young Arthur is my son, and he is lost:
I am not mad, I would to heaven I were,
For then 'tis like I should forget myself:
50 O, if I could, what grief should I forget!
Preach some philosophy to make me mad,
And thou shalt be canónized, cardinal;
For, being not mad but sensible of grief,
My reasonable part produces reason
How I may be delivered of these woes,
And teaches me to kill or hang myself:
If I were mad, I should forget my son,
Or madly think a babe of clouts were he:
I am not mad; too well, too well I feel
60 The different plague of each calamity.

   K. Philip. Bind up those tresses...O, what love I note
In the fair multitude of those her hairs!
Where but by chance a silver drop hath fallen,
Even to that drop ten thousand wiry friends
Do glue themselves in sociable grief,
Like true, inseparable, faithful loves,
Sticking together in calamity.

   Constance. To England, if you will.

   K. Philip.   Bind up your hairs.

   Constance. Yes, that I will; and wherefore will I do it?
70 I tore them from their bonds and cried aloud,
'O that these hands could so redeem my son,
As they have given these hairs their liberty!'
But now I envy at their liberty,
And will again commit them to their bonds,
Because my poor child is a prisoner....

                           [she knits up her hair

And, father cardinal, I have heard you say
That we shall see and know our friends in heaven:
If that be true, I shall see my boy again;

For, since the birth of Cain, the first male child,
To him that did but yesterday suspire,   80
There was not such a gracious creature born:
But now will canker-sorrow eat my bud
And chase the native beauty from his cheek,
And he will look as hollow as a ghost,
As dim and meagre as an ague's fit,
And so he'll die; and, rising so again,
When I shall meet him in the court of heaven
I shall not know him: therefore never, never
Must I behold my pretty Arthur more.
   Pandulph. You hold too heinous a respect of grief. 90
   Constance. He talks to me that never had a son.
   K. Philip. You are as fond of grief as of your child.
   Constance. Grief fills the room up of my absent child:
Lies in his bed, walks up and down with me,
Puts on his pretty looks, repeats his words,
Remembers me of all his gracious parts,
Stuffs out his vacant garments with his form;
Then have I reason to be fond of grief!
Fare you well: had you such a loss as I,
I could give better comfort than you do.   100
I will not keep this form upon my head,
When there is such disorder in my wit...
                           [she tears her hair again
O Lord! my boy, my Arthur, my fair son!
My life, my joy, my food, my all the world!
My widow-comfort, and my sorrows' cure!
                               [she runs forth
   K. Philip. I fear some outrage, and I'll follow her.
                               [he goes
   Lewis. There's nothing in this world can make me joy:
Life is as tedious as a twice-told tale
Vexing the dull ear of a drowsy man;

110 And bitter shame hath spoiled the sweet world's taste,
  That it yields nought but shame and bitterness.
   Pandulph. Before the curing of a strong disease,
  Even in the instant of repair and health,
  The fit is strongest; evils that take leave,
  On their departure most of all show evil:
  What have you lost by losing of this day?
   Lewis. All days of glory, joy and happiness.
   Pandulph. If you had won it, certainly you had.
  No, no: when Fortune means to men most good,
120 She looks upon them with a threat'ning eye:
  'Tis strange to think how much King John hath lost
  In this which he accounts so clearly won:
  Are not you grieved that Arthur is his prisoner?
   Lewis. As heartily as he is glad he hath him.
   Pandulph. Your mind is all as youthful as your blood.
  Now hear me speak with a prophetic spirit;
  For even the breath of what I mean to speak
  Shall blow each dust, each straw, each little rub,
  Out of the path which shall directly lead
130 Thy foot to England's throne: and therefore mark.
  John hath seized Arthur, and it cannot be
  That, whiles warm life plays in that infant's veins,
  The misplaced John should entertain an hour,
  One minute, nay, one quiet breath of rest.
  A sceptre snatched with an unruly hand
  Must be as boisterously maintained as gained;
  And he that stands upon a slippery place
  Makes nice of no vile hold to stay him up:
  That John may stand, then Arthur needs must fall,
140 So be it, for it cannot be but so.
   Lewis. But what shall I gain by young Arthur's fall?
   Pandulph. You, in the right of Lady Blanch your wife,
  May then make all the claim that Arthur did.
   Lewis. And lose it, life and all, as Arthur did.

Pandulph. How green you are, and fresh in this
　　old world!
John lays you plots; the times conspire with you;
For he that steeps his safety in true blood
Shall find but bloody safety and untrue.
This act so evilly borne shall cool the hearts
Of all his people and freeze up their zeal,　　　　150
That none so small advantage shall step forth
To check his reign, but they will cherish it;
No natural exhalation in the sky,
No scope of nature, no distempered day,
No common wind, no customéd event,
But they will pluck away his natural cause,
And call them meteors, prodigies and signs,
Abortives, presages and tongues of heaven,
Plainly denouncing vengeance upon John.
Lewis. May be he will not touch young
　　Arthur's life,　　　　160
But hold himself safe in his prisonment.
Pandulph. O, sir, when he shall hear of
　　your approach,
If that young Arthur be not gone already,
Even at that news he dies; and then the hearts
Of all his people shall revolt from him,
And kiss the lips of unacquainted change,
And pick strong matter of revolt and wrath
Out of the bloody fingers' ends of John....
Methinks I see this hurly all on foot;
And, O, what better matter breeds for you　　　　170
Than I have named! The bastard Faulconbridge
Is now in England, ransacking the church,
Offending charity: if but a dozen French
Were there in arms, they would be as a call
To train ten thousand English to their side;
Or as a little snow, tumbled about,

Anon becomes a mountain....O noble Dauphin,
Go with me to the king. 'Tis wonderful
What may be wrought out of their discontent,
180 Now that their souls are topfull of offence.
For England go! I will whet on the king.

   Lewis. Strong reasons make strong actions: let us go.
If you say ay, the king will not say no.   [*they go*

[4.1.] *England. A room in a castle with an arras upon the
back wall; coals burning in a brazier; a table and chair*

'*Enter* HUBERT *and Executioners' bearing searing irons*

   Hubert. Heat me these irons hot, and look thou stand
Within the arras: when I strike my foot
Upon the bosom of the ground, rush forth,
And bind the boy which you shall find with me
Fast to the chair: be heedful: hence, and watch.

   1 *Executioner.* I hope your warrant will bear out
        the deed.

   Hubert. Uncleanly scruples! fear not you: look to't....
        [*the Executioners stand behind the arras;
         Hubert goes to the door and calls*
Young lad, come forth; I have to say with you.

              ARTHUR *enters*

   Arthur. Good morrow, Hubert.
   Hubert.   Good morrow, little prince.
10 *Arthur.* As little prince, having so great a title
To be more prince, as may be...You are sad.
   Hubert. Indeed, I have been merrier.
   Arthur.   Mercy on me!
Methinks no body should be sad but I:
Yet I remember, when I was in France,
Young gentlemen would be as sad as night,

Only for wantonness: by my christendom,
So I were out of prison and kept sheep,
I should be as merry as the day is long;
And so I would be here, but that I doubt
My uncle practises more harm to me:.   20
He is afraid of me and I of him:
Is it my fault that I was Geffrey's son?
No, indeed is't not; and I would to heaven
I were your son, so you would love me, Hubert.
  (*Hubert.* If I talk to him, with his innocent prate
He will awake my mercy which lies dead:
Therefore I will be sudden and dispatch.
  Arthur. Are you sick, Hubert? you look pale to-day.
In sooth, I would you were a little sick,
That I might sit all night and watch with you.   30
I warrant I love you more than you do me.
  (*Hubert.* His words do take possession of my bosom....
[*he shows a paper*] Read here, young Arthur....
                    [*aside*] How now, foolish rheum!
Turning dispiteous torture out of door!
I must be brief, lest resolution drop
Out at mine eyes in tender womanish tears....
Can you not read it? is it not fair writ?
  Arthur. Too fairly, Hubert, for so foul effect.
Must you, with hot irons, burn out both mine eyes?
  Hubert. Young boy, I must.
  Arthur.   And will you?
  Hubert.   And I will. 40
  Arthur. Have you the heart? When your head did
          but ache,
I knit my handkercher about your brows,
(The best I had, a princess wrought it me)
And I did never ask it you again:
And with my hand at midnight held your head;

And like the watchful minutes to the hour,
Still and anon cheered up the heavy time;
Saying, 'What lack you?' and 'Where lies your grief?'
Or 'What good love may I perform for you?'
50 Many a poor man's son would have lien still,
And ne'er have spoke a loving word to you;
But you at your sick service had a prince:
Nay, you may think my love was crafty love,
And call it cunning: do, an if you will:
If heaven be pleased that you must use me ill,
Why then you must....Will you put out mine eyes?
These eyes that never did nor never shall
So much as frown on you?
    Hubert.   I have sworn to do it;
And with hot irons must I burn them out.
60   *Arthur.* Ah, none but in this iron age would do it!
The iron of itself, though heat red-hot,
Approaching near these eyes, would drink my tears,
And quench his fiery indignation,
Even in the matter of mine innocence:
Nay, after that, consume away in rust,
But for containing fire to harm mine eye:
Are you more stubborn-hard than hammered iron?
An if an angel should have come to me,
And told me Hubert should put out mine eyes,
70 I would not have believed him...no tongue but
        Hubert's!
    Hubert. [*stamps on the ground*] Come forth.

    The Executioners come forth with cord, irons, &c.

Do as I bid you do.
    Arthur. O, save me, Hubert, save me! my eyes are out,
Even with the fierce looks of these bloody men.
    Hubert. Give me the iron, I say, and bind him here.
                              [*they sieze him*

Arthur. Alas, what need you be so boist'rous-rough?
I will not struggle, I will stand stone-still:
For heaven sake, Hubert, let me not be bound!
Nay, hear me, Hubert, drive these men away,
And I will sit as quiet as a lamb;   80
I will not stir, not wince, nor speak a word,
Nor look upon the iron angerly:
Thrust but these men away, and I'll forgive you,
Whatever torment you do put to me.

  Hubert. Go, stand within: let me alone with him.

  1 *Executioner.* I am best pleased to be from such
     a deed.   [*the Executioners go out, leaving an
                     iron upon the table*

  Arthur. Alas! I then have chid away my friend!
He hath a stern look, but a gentle heart:
Let him come back, that his compassion may
Give life to yours.

  Hubert.   Come, boy, prepare yourself.   90

  Arthur. Is there no remedy?

  Hubert.   None, but to lose your eyes.

  Arthur. O heaven! that there were but a mote in
     yours,
A grain, a dust, a gnat, a wandering hair,
Any annoyance in that precious sense!
Then, feeling what small things are boisterous there,
Your vile intent must needs seem horrible.

  Hubert. Is this your promise? go to, hold your
     tongue.

  Arthur. Hubert, the utterance of a brace of tongues
Must needs want pleading for a pair of eyes:
Let me not hold my tongue; let me not, Hubert!   100
Or, Hubert, if you will, cut out my tongue,
So I may keep mine eyes....O, spare mine eyes,
Though to no use, but still to look on you!
                     [*he snatches up the iron*

Lo, by my troth, the instrument is cold,
And would not harm me.
   Hubert.   I can heat it, boy.
   Arthur. No, in good sooth; the fire is dead with grief,
Being create for comfort, to be used
In undeserved extremes: see else yourself,
There is no malice in this burning coal,
110 The breath of heaven hath blown his spirit out,
And strewed repentant ashes on his head.
   Hubert. But with my breath I can revive it, boy.
   Arthur. An if you do, you will but make it blush,
And glow with shame of your proceedings, Hubert:
Nay, it perchance will sparkle in your eyes;
And like a dog that is compelled to fight,
Snatch at his master that doth tarre him on.
All things that you should use to do me wrong
Deny their office: only you do lack
120 That mercy which fierce fire and iron extend,
Creatures of note for mercy-lacking uses.
   Hubert. Well, see to live; I will not touch thine eyes
For all the treasure that thine uncle owes.
Yet am I sworn, and I did purpose, boy,
With this same very iron to burn them out.
   Arthur. O, now you look like Hubert! all this while
You were disguiséd.
   Hubert.   Peace: no more. Adieu.
Your uncle must not know but you are dead.
I'll fill these doggéd spies with false reports:
130 And, pretty child, sleep doubtless and secure,
That Hubert, for the wealth of all the world,
Will not offend thee.
   Arthur.   O heaven! I thank you, Hubert.
   Hubert. Silence, no more: go closely in with me.
Much danger do I undergo for thee.   *[they go*

[4. 2.]   *King John's palace*

*KING JOHN crowned and enthroned in full state, with
  PEMBROKE, SALISBURY and other lords about him*

  K. John. Here once again we sit; once again crowned,
And looked upon, I hope, with cheerful eyes.
  Pembroke. This 'once again' (but that your
          highness pleased)
Was once superfluous: you were crowned before,
And that high royalty was ne'er plucked off;
The faiths of men ne'er stainéd with revolt;
Fresh expectation troubled not the land,
With any longed-for change or better state.
  Salisbury. Therefore, to be possessed with
          double pomp,
To guard a title that was rich before,   10
To gild refinéd gold, to paint the lily,
To throw a perfume on the violet,
To smooth the ice, or add another hue
Unto the rainbow, or with taper-light
To seek the beauteous eye of heaven to garnish,
Is wasteful and ridiculous excess.
  Pembroke. But that your royal pleasure must be done,
This act is as an ancient tale new told,
And in the last repeating troublesome,
Being urgéd at a time unseasonable.   20
  Salisbury. In this the antique and well noted face
Of plain old form is much disfiguréd,
And like a shifted wind unto a sail,
It makes the course of thoughts to fetch about,
Startles and frights consideration,
Makes sound opinion sick and truth suspected,
For putting on so new a fashioned robe.

Pembroke. When workmen strive to do better than well,
They do confound their skill in covetousness,
30 And oftentimes excusing of a fault
Doth make the fault the worse by the excuse;
As patches set upon a little breach
Discredit more in hiding of the fault
Than did the fault before it was so patched.

Salisbury. To this effect, before you were new crowned,
We breathed our counsel: but it pleased your highness
To overbear it, and we are all well pleased,
Since all and every part of what we would
Doth make a stand at what your highness will.

40 *K. John.* Some reasons of this double coronation
I have possessed you with and think them strong;
†And more, more strong when lesser is my fear,
I shall indue you with: meantime but ask
What you would have reformed that is not well,
And well shall you perceive how willingly
I will both hear and grant you your requests.

Pembroke. Then I, as one that am the tongue of these,
To sound the purposes of all their hearts,
Both for myself and them...but, chief of all,
50 Your safety...for the which myself and they
Bend their best studies, heartily request
Th'enfranchisement of Arthur, whose restraint
Doth move the murmuring lips of discontent
To break into this dangerous argument,—
If what in rest you have in right you hold,
Why then your fears, which as they say attend
The steps of wrong, should move you to mew up
Your tender kinsman, and to choke his days
With barbarous ignorance, and deny his youth
60 The rich advantage of good exercise.
That the time's enemies may not have this

To grace occasions, let it be our suit
That you have bid us ask his liberty,
Which for our goods we do no further ask
Than whereupon our weal, on you depending,
Counts it your weal he have his liberty.

HUBERT enters

  K. John. Let it be so: I do commit his youth
To your direction....Hubert, what news with you?
                      [they talk apart
  Pembroke. This is the man should do the bloody deed;
He showed his warrant to a friend of mine.   70
The image of a wicked heinous fault
Lives in his eye; that close aspect of his
Doth show the mood of a much troubled breast,
And I do fearfully believe 'tis done,
What we so feared he had a charge to do.
  Salisbury. The colour of the king doth come and go
Between his purpose and his conscience,
Like heralds 'twixt two dreadful battles set:
His passion is so ripe, it needs must break.
  Pembroke. And when it breaks, I fear will issue thence 80
The foul corruption of a sweet child's death.
  K. John [*to Hubert, aloud*]. We cannot hold mor-
      tality's strong hand...
Good lords, although my will to give is living,
The suit which you demand is gone and dead.
He tells us Arthur is deceased to-night.
  Salisbury. Indeed we feared his sickness was past cure.
  Pembroke. Indeed we heard how near his death he was,
Before the child himself felt he was sick:
This must be answered either here or hence.
  K. John. Why do you bend such solemn brows
      on me?
                         90

Think you I bear the shears of destiny?
Have I commandment on the pulse of life?
  Salisbury. It is apparent foul-play, and 'tis shame
That greatness should so grossly offer it:
So thrive it in your game! and so farewell.
  Pembroke. Stay yet, Lord Salisbury, I'll go with thee,
And find th'inheritance of this poor child,
His little kingdom of a forcéd grave.
That blood which owed the breadth of all this isle,
100 Three foot of it doth hold: bad world the while!
This must not be thus borne: this will break out
To all our sorrows, and ere long I doubt.
                          [*the Lords depart*
  (*K. John.* They burn in indignation...I repent...
There is no sure foundation set on blood...
No certain life achieved by others' death...

A Messenger enters

A fearful eye thou hast. Where is that blood
That I have seen inhabit in those cheeks?
So foul a sky clears not without a storm.
Pour down thy weather: how goes all in France?
110 *Messenger.* From France to England. Never such
      a power
For any foreign preparation
Was levied in the body of a land!
The copy of your speed is learned by them;
For when you should be told they do prepare,
The tidings comes that they are all arrived.
  K. John. O, where hath our intelligence been drunk?
Where hath it slept? Where is my mother's care,
That such an army could be drawn in France,
And she not hear of it?
  Messenger.   My liege, her ear

Is stopped with dust: the first of April died   120
Your noble mother; and as I hear, my lord,
The Lady Constance in a frenzy died
Three days before: but this from rumour's tongue
I idly heard; if true or false I know not.
  K. John. Withhold thy speed, dreadful occasion!
O, make a league with me, till I have pleased
My discontented peers! What! mother dead!
How wildly then walks my estate in France!
Under whose conduct came those powers of France
That thou for truth giv'st out are landed here?   130
  Messenger. Under the Dauphin.
  K. John.   Thou hast made me giddy
With these ill tidings...

        The BASTARD enters with PETER of Pomfret

                    Now, what says the world
To your proceedings? do not seek to stuff
My head with more ill news, for it is full.
  Bastard. But if you be afeard to hear the worst,
Then let the worst unheard fall on your head.
  K. John. Bear with me, cousin, for I was amazed
Under the tide; but now I breathe again
Aloft the flood, and can give audience
To any tongue, speak it of what it will.   140
  Bastard. How I have sped among the clergymen,
The sums I have collected shall express:
But as I travelled hither through the land,
I find the people strangely fantasied,
Possessed with rumours, full of idle dreams,
Not knowing what they fear, but full of fear.
And here's a prophet, that I brought with me
From forth the streets of Pomfret, whom I found
With many hundreds treading on his heels;

5   PSKJ

150 To whom he sung, in rude harsh-sounding rhymes,
That, ere the next Ascension-day at noon,
Your highness should deliver up your crown.
  K. John. Thou idle dreamer, wherefore didst thou so?
  Peter. Foreknowing that the truth will fall out so.
  K. John. Hubert, away with him! imprison him,
And on that day at noon, whereon he says
I shall yield up my crown, let him be hanged.
Deliver him to safety, and return,
For I must use thee....   *[Hubert takes Peter away*
                              O my gentle cousin,
Hear'st thou the news abroad, who are arrived?
160 *Bastard.* The French, my lord. Men's mouths are
    full of it:
Besides, I met Lord Bigot and Lord Salisbury,
With eyes as red as new-enkindled fire,
And others more, going to seek the grave
Of Arthur, whom they say is killed to-night
On your suggestion.
  K. John.   Gentle kinsman, go,
And thrust thyself into their companies.
I have a way to win their loves again;
Bring them before me.
  Bastard.   I will seek them out.
  K. John. Nay, but make haste; the better foot before.
170 O, let me have no subject enemies,
When adverse foreigners affright my towns
With dreadful pomp of stout invasion!
Be Mercury, set feathers to thy heels,
And fly—like thought—from them to me again.
  Bastard. The spirit of the time shall teach me speed.
  K. John. Spoke like a sprightful noble gentleman....
                                        [he goes
[to the Messenger] Go after him; for he perhaps
    shall need

Some messenger betwixt me and the peers,
And be thou he.
  Messenger.   With all my heart, my liege. [*he goes* 180
  K. John. My mother dead!

HUBERT returns

  Hubert. My lord, they say five moons were seen tonight:
Four fixéd, and the fifth did whirl about
The other four in wondrous motion.
  K. John. Five moons!
  Hubert.   Old men and beldams in the streets
Do prophesy upon it dangerously:
Young Arthur's death is common in their mouths,
And when they talk of him, they shake their heads
And whisper one another in the ear;
And he that speaks doth gripe the hearer's wrist,   190
Whilst he that hears makes fearful action,
With wrinkled brows, with nods, with rolling eyes.
I saw a smith stand with his hammer, thus,
The whilst his iron did on the anvil cool,
With open mouth swallowing a tailor's news,
Who with his shears and measure in his hand,
Standing on slippers, which his nimble haste
Had falsely thrust upon contrary feet,
Told of a many thousand warlike French
That were embattléd and ranked in Kent: 200
Another lean unwashed artificer
Cuts off his tale and talks of Arthur's death.
  K. John. Why seek'st thou to possess me with
    these fears?
Why urgest thou so oft young Arthur's death?
Thy hand hath murdered him: I had a mighty cause
To wish him dead, but thou hadst none to kill him.
  Hubert. No had, my lord? why, did you not
    provoke me?

K. John. It is the curse of kings to be attended
By slaves that take their humours for a warrant
210 To break within the bloody house of life,
And on the winking of authority
To understand a law; to know the meaning
Of dangerous majesty, when perchance it frowns
More upon humour than advised respect.
   Hubert. [*shows the warrant*] Here is your hand and
     seal for what I did.
   K. John. O, when the last account 'twixt heaven
     and earth
Is to be made, then shall this hand and seal
Witness against us to damnation!
How oft the sight of means to do ill deeds
220 Make deeds ill done! Hadst not thou been by,
A fellow by the hand of nature marked,
Quoted and signed to do a deed of shame,
This murder had not come into my mind:
But taking note of thy abhorred aspect,
Finding thee fit for bloody villany,
Apt, liable to be employed in danger,
I faintly broke with thee of Arthur's death;
And thou, to be endearéd to a king,
Made it no conscience to destroy a prince.
230 *Hubert.* My lord—
   K. John. Hadst thou but shook thy head or made
     a pause
When I spake darkly what I purposéd,
Or turned an eye of doubt upon my face,
As bid me tell my tale in express words,
Deep shame had struck me dumb, made me break off,
And those thy fears might have wrought fears in me:
But thou didst understand me by my signs
And didst in signs again parley with sin;

Yea, without stop, didst let thy heart consent,
And consequently thy rude hand to act   240
The deed, which both our tongues held vile to name....
Out of my sight, and never see me more!
My nobles leave me, and my state is braved,
Even at my gates, with ranks of foreign powers:
Nay, in the body of this fleshly land, [*strikes his breast*
This kingdom, this confine of blood and breath,
Hostility and civil tumult reigns
Between my conscience and my cousin's death.

  Hubert. Arm you against your other enemies,
I'll make a peace between your soul and you.   250
Young Arthur is alive: this hand of mine
Is yet a maiden and an innocent hand,
Not painted with the crimson spots of blood.
Within this bosom never entered yet
The dreadful motion of a murderous thought,
And you have slandered nature in my form,
Which, howsoever rude exteriorly,
Is yet the cover of a fairer mind
Than to be butcher of an innocent child.

  K. John. Doth Arthur live? O, haste thee to
     the peers,   260
Throw this report on their incensèd rage,
And make them tame to their obedience!
Forgive the comment that my passion made
Upon thy feature, for my rage was blind,
And foul imaginary eyes of blood
Presented thee more hideous than thou art.
O, answer not; but to my closet bring
The angry lords, with all expedient haste.
I conjure thee but slowly; run more fast.   [*they go*

[4. 3.] *Before the castle*

ARTHUR appears on the walls

Arthur. The wall is high, and yet will I leap down.
Good ground, be pitiful and hurt me not!
There's few or none do know me—if they did,
This ship-boy's semblance hath disguised me quite....
I am afraid, and yet I'll venture it....
If I get down, and do not break my limbs,
I'll find a thousand shifts to get away:
As good to die and go, as die and stay....   [*he leaps*
O me! my uncle's spirit is in these stones.
10 Heaven take my soul, and England keep my bones!
                                                    [*he 'dies*]

PEMBROKE, SALISBURY, and BIGOT come up talking

Salisbury. Lords, I will meet him at Saint
        Edmundsbury.
It is our safety, and we must embrace
This gentle offer of the perilous time.
Pembroke. Who brought that letter from the cardinal?
Salisbury. The Count Melun, a noble lord of France;
Whose private with me of the Dauphin's love
Is much more general than these lines import.
Bigot. To-morrow morning let us meet him then.
Salisbury. Or rather then set forward, for 'twill be
20 Two long days' journey, lords, or ere we meet.

The BASTARD approaches

Bastard. Once more to-day well met, distempered lords!
The king by me requests your presence straight.
Salisbury. The king hath dispossessed himself of us.
We will not line his thin bestainéd cloak

With our pure honours, nor attend the foot
That leaves the print of blood where'er it walks.
Return and tell him so: we know the worst.

   Bastard. Whate'er you think, good words, I think,
     were best.

   Salisbury. Our griefs, and not our manners, reason now.

   Bastard. But there is little reason in your grief,   30
Therefore 'twere reason you had manners now.

   Pembroke. Sir, sir, impatience hath his privilege.

   Bastard. 'Tis true, to hurt his master, no man else.

   Salisbury. This is the prison…[*sees Arthur*] What is
     he lies here?

   Pembroke. O death, made proud with pure and
     princely beauty!
The earth had not a hole to hide this deed.

   Salisbury. Murder, as hating what himself hath done,
Doth lay it open to urge on revenge.

   Bigot. Or, when he doomed this beauty to a grave,
Found it too precious-princely for a grave.   40

   Salisbury. Sir Richard, what think you? have
     you beheld,
Or have you read or heard? or could you think?
Or do you almost think, although you see,
That you do see? could thought, without this object,
Form such another? This is the very top,
The height, the crest, or crest unto the crest,
Of murder's arms: this is the bloodiest shame,
The wildest savagery, the vilest stroke,
That ever wall-eyed wrath or staring rage
Presented to the tears of soft remorse.   50

   Pembroke. All murders past do stand excused in this:
And this, so sole and so unmatchable,
Shall give a holiness, a purity,
To the yet unbegotten sin of times;

And prove a deadly bloodshed but a jest,
Exampled by this heinous spectacle.
　　Bastard. It is a damnéd and a bloody work,
The graceless action of a heavy hand,
If that it be the work of any hand.
60　*Salisbury.* If that it be the work of any hand!
We had a kind of light what would ensue:
It is the shameful work of Hubert's hand,
The practice and the purpose of the king:　　[*he kneels*
From whose obedience I forbid my soul,
Kneeling before this ruin of sweet life,
And breathing to his breathless excellence
The incense of a vow, a holy vow,
Never to taste the pleasures of the world,
Never to be infected with delight,
70　Nor conversant with ease and idleness,
Till I have set a glory to this hand,
By giving it the worship of revenge.
　　Pembroke. Bigot. Our souls religiously confirm
　　thy words.

Hubert comes up

　　Hubert. Lords, I am hot with haste in seeking you,
Arthur doth live, the king hath sent for you.
　　Salisbury. O, he is bold, and blushes not at death.
Avaunt, thou hateful villain, get thee gone!
　　Hubert. I am no villain.
　　Salisbury. [*draws his sword*]　Must I rob the law?
　　Bastard. Your sword is bright, sir, put it up again.
80　*Salisbury.* Not till I sheathe it in a murderer's skin.
　　Hubert. Stand back, Lord Salisbury, stand back, I say;
By heaven, I think my sword's as sharp as yours.
I would not have you, lord, forget yourself,
Nor tempt the danger of my true defence;

Lest I, by marking of your rage, forget
Your worth, your greatness, and nobility.
  Bigot. Out, dunghill! dar'st thou brave a nobleman?
  Hubert. Not for my life: but yet I dare defend
My innocent life against an emperor.
  Salisbury. Thou art a murderer.
  Hubert.   Do not prove me so; 90
Yet I am none. Whose tongue soe'er speaks false,
Not truly speaks; who speaks not truly, lies.
  Pembroke. Cut him to pieces.
  Bastard.   Keep the peace, I say.
  Salisbury. Stand by, or I shall gall you, Faulconbridge.
  Bastard. Thou wert better gall the devil, Salisbury.
If thou but frown on me, or stir thy foot,
Or teach thy hasty spleen to do me shame,
I'll strike thee dead. Put up thy sword betime,
Or I'll so maul you and your toasting-iron,
That you shall think the devil is come from hell.   100
  Bigot. What wilt thou do, renownèd Faulconbridge?
Second a villain and a murderer?
  Hubert. Lord Bigot, I am none.
  Bigot. [*points*]   Who killed this prince?
  Hubert. [*sees the body for the first time*] 'Tis not an
        hour since I left him well: [*he kneels*
I honoured him, I loved him, and will weep
My date of life out for his sweet life's loss.
  Salisbury. Trust not those cunning waters of his eyes,
For villany is not without such rheum,
And he, long traded in it, makes it seem
Like rivers of remorse and innocency.   110
Away, with me, all you whose souls abhor
Th'uncleanly savours of a slaughter-house,
For I am stifled with this smell of sin.
  Bigot. Away toward Bury, to the Dauphin there!

Pembroke. There, tell the king, he may inquire us out.

[*the Lords depart*

Bastard. Here's a good world! Knew you of this
    fair work?
Beyond the infinite and boundless reach
Of mercy (if thou didst this deed of death)
Art thou damned, Hubert.

    Hubert.   Do but hear me, sir.

120 *Bastard.* Ha! I'll tell thee what;
Thou'rt damned as black—nay, nothing is so black.
Thou art more deep damned than Prince Lucifer:
There is not yet so ugly a fiend of hell
As thou shalt be, if thou didst kill this child.

    Hubert. Upon my soul—

    Bastard.   If thou didst but consent
To this most cruel act, do but despair,
And if thou want'st a cord, the smallest thread
That ever spider twisted from her womb
Will serve to strangle thee; a rush will be a beam

130 To hang thee on; or, wouldst thou drown thyself,
Put but a little water in a spoon,
And it shall be as all the ocean,
Enough to stifle such a villain up.
I do suspect thee very grievously.

    Hubert. If I in act, consent, or sin of thought,
Be guilty of the stealing that sweet breath
Which was embounded in this beauteous clay,
Let hell want pains enough to torture me...
I left him well.

    Bastard.   Go, bear him in thine arms:

[*Hubert takes up the body*

140 I am amazed, methinks, and lose my way
Among the thorns and dangers of this world.
How easy dost thou take all England up

From forth this morsel of dead royalty,
The life, the right and truth of all this realm
Is fled to heaven; and England now is left
To tug and scamble, and to part by th'teeth
The unowed interest of proud-swelling state:
Now, for the bare-picked bone of majesty,
Doth doggéd war bristle his angry crest,
And snarleth in the gentle eyes of peace: 　　　　150
Now powers from home and discontents at home
Meet in one line; and vast confusion waits,
As doth a raven on a sick-fall'n beast,
The imminent decay of wrested pomp.
Now happy he whose cloak and centure can
Hold out this tempest. Bear away that child,
And follow me with speed; I'll to the king:
A thousand businesses are brief in hand,
And heaven itself doth frown upon the land. [*they go*

[5. 1.]　　　　*King John's palace*

Pandulph enthroned, holds the crown of England in his
hands; King John kneels before him; Lords and others
in attendance

　K. *John.* Thus have I yielded up into your hand
The circle of my glory.
　Pandulph. [*places the crown upon John's head*]
　　　　　　　　Take again
From this my hand, as holding of the Pope,
Your sovereign greatness and authority.
　K. *John.* [*rises*] Now keep your holy word, go meet
　　the French,
And from his holiness use all your power
To stop their marches 'fore we are inflamed:

Our discontented counties do revolt;
Our people quarrel with obedience,
10 Swearing allegiance and the love of soul
To stranger blood, to foreign royalty:
This inundation of mistempered humour
Rests by you only to be qualified.
Then pause not; for the present time's so sick,
That present medicine must be ministered,
Or overthrow incurable ensues.
    Pandulph. It was my breath that blew this tempest up,
Upon your stubborn usage of the Pope;
But since you are a gentle convertite,
20 My tongue shall hush again this storm of war,
And make fair weather in your blust'ring land...
On this Ascension-day, remember well,
Upon your oath of service to the Pope,
Go I to make the French lay down their arms.
                            [he departs
    K. John. Is this Ascension-day? Did not the prophet
Say that before Ascension-day at noon
My crown I should give off? Even so I have:
I did suppose it should be on constraint,
But, heaven be thanked, it is but voluntary.

The BASTARD enters

30   *Bastard.* All Kent hath yielded; nothing there holds out
But Dover castle: London hath received,
Like a kind host, the Dauphin and his powers:
Your nobles will not hear you, but are gone
To offer service to your enemy;
And wild amazement hurries up and down
The little number of your doubtful friends.
    K. John. Would not my lords return to me again,
After they heard young Arthur was alive?

Bastard. They found him dead and cast into the streets,
An empty casket, where the jewel of life　　　　　40
By some damned hand was robbed and ta'en away.

K. John. That villain Hubert told me he did live.

Bastard. So, on my soul, he did, for aught he knew...
But wherefore do you droop? why look you sad?
Be great in act, as you have been in thought;
Let not the world see fear and sad distrust
Govern the motion of a kingly eye:
Be stirring as the time, be fire with fire,
Threaten the threat'ner, and outface the brow
Of bragging horror: so shall inferior eyes,　　　　　50
That borrow their behaviours from the great,
Grow great by your example and put on
The dauntless spirit of resolution....
Away, and glister like the god of war,
When he intendeth to become the field:
Show boldness and aspiring confidence:
What, shall they seek the lion in his den?
And fright him there? and make him tremble there?
O, let it not be said: forage, and run
To meet displeasure farther from the doors,　　　　　60
And grapple with him, ere he come so nigh.

K. John. The legate of the Pope hath been with me,
And I have made a happy peace with him,
And he hath promised to dismiss the powers
Led by the Dauphin.

Bastard.　　　　　O inglorious league!
Shall we, upon the footing of our land,
Send fair-play orders and make compromise,
Insinuation, parley and base truce
To arms invasive? shall a beardless boy,
A cock'red silken wanton, brave our fields,　　　　　70
And flesh his spirit in a warlike soil,

Mocking the air with colours idly spread,
And find no check? Let us, my liege, to arms:
Perchance the cardinal cannot make your peace;
Or if he do, let it at least be said
They saw we had a purpose of defence.

    K. John. Have thou the ordering of this present time.

    Bastard. Away then, with good courage! yet, I know,
Our party may well meet a prouder foe.   *[they go*

[5. 2.] *The DAUPHIN's camp near St Edmundsbury*

'*Enter, in arms,* LEWIS, SALISBURY, MELUN,
PEMBROKE, BIGOT, *Soldiers*'

    Lewis. My Lord Melun, let this be copied out,
And keep it safe for our remembrance:
Return the precedent to these lords again,
That, having our fair order written down,
Both they and we, perusing o'er these notes,
May know wherefore we took the sacrament
And keep our faiths firm and inviolable.

    Salisbury. Upon our sides it never shall be broken.
And, noble Dauphin, albeit we swear
10 A voluntary zeal and an unurgéd faith
To your proceedings; yet believe me, prince,
I am not glad that such a sore of time
Should seek a plaster by contemned revolt,
And heal the inveterate canker of one wound
By making many: O, it grieves my soul,
That I must draw this metal from my side
To be a widow-maker! O, and there
Where honourable rescue and defence
Cries out upon the name of Salisbury!
20 But such is the infection of the time,

That, for the health and physic of our right,
We cannot deal but with the very hand
Of stern injustice and confuséd wrong:
And is't not pity, O my grievéd friends,
That we, the sons and children of this isle,
Were born to see so sad an hour as this,
Wherein we step after a stranger, march
Upon her gentle bosom, and fill up
Her enemies' ranks—I must withdraw and weep
Upon the spot of this enforcéd cause—   30
To grace the gentry of a land remote,
And follow unacquainted colours here?
What, here? O nation, that thou could'st remove!
That Neptune's arms, who clippeth thee about,
Would bear thee from the knowledge of thyself,
And grapple thee unto a pagan shore,
Where these two Christian armies might combine
The blood of malice in a vein of league,
And not to spend it so unneighbourly!
    Lewis. A noble temper dost thou show in this;   40
And great affections wrastling in thy bosom
Doth make an earthquake of nobility:
O, what a noble combat hast thou fought,
Between compulsion and a brave respect!
Let me wipe off this honourable dew,
That silverly doth progress on thy cheeks:
My heart hath melted at a lady's tears,
Being an ordinary inundation;
But this effusion of such manly drops,
This shower, blown up by tempest of the soul,   50
Startles mine eyes, and makes me more amazed
Than had I seen the vaulty top of heaven
Figured quite o'er with burning meteors.
Lift up thy brow, renownéd Salisbury,

And with a great heart heave away this storm:
Commend these waters to those baby eyes
That never saw the giant world enraged,
Nor met with fortune other than at feasts,
Full of warm blood, of mirth, of gossiping:
60 Come, come; for thou shalt thrust thy hand as deep
Into the purse of rich prosperity
As Lewis himself: so, nobles, shall you all,
That knit your sinews to the strength of mine....

                              [*a trumpet sounds*

And even there, methinks, an angel spake.

PANDULPH *approaches with his train*

Look, where the holy legate comes apace,
To give us warrant from the hand of heaven,
And on our actions set the name of right
With holy breath.
    Pandulph.   Hail, noble prince of France!
The next is this: King John hath reconciled
70 Himself to Rome, his spirit is come in,
That so stood out against the holy church,
The great metropolis and see of Rome:
Therefore thy threat'ning colours now wind up,
And tame the savage spirit of wild war,
That, like a lion fostered up at hand,
It may lie gently at the foot of peace,
And be no further harmful than in show.
    Lewis. Your grace shall pardon me, I will not back:
I am too high-born to be propertied,
80 To be a secondary at control,
Or useful serving-man and instrument
To any sovereign state throughout the world.
Your breath first kindled the dead coal of wars
Between this chastised kingdom and myself,

And brought in matter that should feed this fire;
And now 'tis far too huge to be blown out
With that same weak wind which enkindled it:
You taught me how to know the face of right,
Acquainted me with interest to this land,
Yea, thrust this enterprise into my heart,   90
And come ye now to tell me John hath made
His peace with Rome? What is that peace to me?
I, by the honour of my marriage-bed,
After young Arthur, claim this land for mine,
And now it is half-conquered must I back,
Because that John hath made his peace with Rome?
Am I Rome's slave? What penny hath Rome borne,
What men provided, what munition sent,
To underprop this action? Is't not I
That undergo this charge? who else but I,   100
And such as to my claim are liable,
Sweat in this business and maintain this war?
Have I not heard these islanders shout out,
'Vive le roy!' as I have banked their towns?
Have I not here the best cards for the game,
To win this easy match played for a crown ⟩
And shall I now give o'er the yielded set?
No, no, on my soul, it never shall be said.
    Pandulph. You look but on the outside of this work.
    Lewis. Outside or inside, I will not return   110
Till my attempt so much be glorified
As to my ample hope was promiséd
Before I drew this gallant head of war,
And culled these fiery spirits from the world,
To outlook conquest and to win renown
Even in the jaws of danger and of death...
                              [*a loud blast from a trumpet*
What lusty trumpet thus doth summon us?
    6   PSKJ

The BASTARD comes up, attended by officers

Bastard. According to the fair-play of the world,
Let me have audience; I am sent to speak:
120 My holy lord of Milan, from the king
I come, to learn how you have dealt for him;
And, as you answer, I do know the scope
And warrant limited unto my tongue.
       Pandulph. The Dauphin is too wilful-opposite,
And will not temporize with my entreaties;
He flatly says he'll not lay down his arms.
       Bastard. By all the blood that ever fury breathed,
The youth says well....Now hear our English king
For thus his royalty doth speak in me:
130 He is prepared, and reason too he should.
This apish and unmannerly approach,
This harnessed masque and unadviséd revel,
This unhaired sauciness and boyish troops,
The king doth smile at, and is well prepared
To whip this dwarfish war, these pigmy arms,
From out the circle of his territories.
That hand which had the strength, even at your door,
To cudgel you and make you take the hatch,
To dive like buckets in concealéd wells,
140 To crouch in litter of your stable planks,
To lie like pawns locked up in chests and trunks,
To hug with swine, to seek sweet safety out
In vaults and prisons, and to thrill and shake
Even at the crying of your nation's crow,
Thinking his voice an arméd Englishman;
Shall that victorious hand be feebled here,
That in your chambers gave you chastisement?
No: know, the gallant monarch is in arms,
And like an eagle o'er his aery towers,

To souse annoyance that comes near his nest...   150
And you degenerate, you ingrate revolts,
You bloody Neroes, ripping up the womb
Of your dear mother England, blush for shame:
For your own ladies and pale-visaged maids
Like Amazons come tripping after drums,
Their thimbles into arméd gauntlets change,
Their needles to lances, and their gentle hearts
To fierce and bloody inclination.
   Lewis. There end thy brave, and turn thy face in peace.
We grant thou canst outscold us: fare thee well.   160
We hold our time too precious to be spent
With such a brabbler.
   Pandulph.   Give me leave to speak.
   Bastard. No, I will speak.
   Lewis.   We will attend to neither...
Strike up the drums, and let the tongue of war
Plead for our interest and our being here.
   Bastard. Indeed, your drums, being beaten, will
       cry out;
And so shall you, being beaten: do but start
An echo with the clamour of thy drum,
And even at hand a drum is ready braced
That shall reverberate all as loud as thine;   170
Sound but another, and another shall
(As loud as thine) rattle the welkin's ear,
And mock the deep-mouthed thunder: for at hand
(Not trusting to this halting legate here,
Whom he hath used rather for sport than need)
Is warlike John; and in his forehead sits
A bare-ribbed death, whose office is this day
To feast upon whole thousands of the French.
   Lewis. Strike up our drums, to find this danger out.
   Bastard. And thou shalt find it, Dauphin, do not doubt. 180
                      [they go

[5. 3.]   *The field of battle*

'Alarums. Enter KING JOHN and HUBERT'

K. John. How goes the day with us? O, tell
    me, Hubert.
Hubert. Badly, I fear: how fares your majesty?
K. John. This fever, that hath troubled me so long,
Lies heavy on me; O, my heart is sick!

A Messenger runs up

Messenger. My lord, your valiant kinsman,
    Faulconbridge,
Desires your majesty to leave the field,
And send him word by me which way you go.
K. John. Tell him, toward Swinstead, to the
    abbey there.
Messenger. Be of good comfort; for the great supply
10 That were expected by the Dauphin here,
Are wracked three nights ago on Goodwin Sands.
This news was brought to Richard but even now.
The French fight coldly, and retire themselves.
    K. John. Ay me! this tyrant fever burns me up,
And will not let me welcome this good news.
Set on toward Swinstead: to my litter straight,
Weakness possesseth me, and I am faint.   [*they go*

[5. 4.]   *SALISBURY, PEMBROKE, and BIGOT pass by*

Salisbury. I did not think the king so stored with friends.
Pembroke. Up once again: put spirit in the French.
If they miscarry, we miscarry too.
Salisbury. That misbegotten devil, Faulconbridge,
In spite of spite, alone upholds the day.
Pembroke. They say King John sore sick hath left
    the field.

Soldiers draw near supporting '*MELUN, wounded*'

Melun.   Lead me to the revolts of England here.
Salisbury.   When we were happy we had other names.
Pembroke.   It is the Count Melun.
Salisbury.   Wounded to death.
Melun.   Fly, noble English, you are bought and sold,   10
Unthread the rude eye of rebellion,
And welcome home again discarded faith.
Seek out King John and fall before his feet;
For if the French be lord of this loud day,
He means to recompense the pains you take
By cutting off your heads: thus hath he sworn,
And I with him, and many moe with me,
Upon the altar at Saint Edmundsbury,
Even on that altar where we swore to you
Dear amity and everlasting love.   20
   Salisbury.   May this be possible? may this be true?
   Melun.   Have I not hideous death within my view,
Retaining but a quantity of life,
Which bleeds away, even as a form of wax
Resolveth from his figure 'gainst the fire?
What in the world should make me now deceive,
Since I must lose the use of all deceit?
Why should I then be false, since it is true
That I must die here and live hence by Truth?
I say again, if Lewis do win the day,   30
He is forsworn, if e'er those eyes of yours
Behold another day break in the east:
But even this night, whose black contagious breath
Already smokes about the burning crest
Of the old, feeble and day-wearied sun,
Even this ill night, your breathing shall expire,
Paying the fine of rated treachery,

Even with a treacherous fine of all your lives,
If Lewis by your assistance win the day....
40 Commend me to one Hubert, with your king;
The love of him, and this respect besides,
For that my grandsire was an Englishman,
Awakes my conscience to confess all this....
In lieu whereof, I pray you, bear me hence
From forth the noise and rumour of the field,
Where I may think the remnant of my thoughts
In peace, and part this body and my soul
With contemplation and devout desires.

    Salisbury. We do believe thee—and beshrew my soul
50 But I do love the favour and the form
Of this most fair occasion, by the which
We will untread the steps of damnéd flight,
And like a bated and retired flood,
Leaving our rankness and irregular course,
Stoop low within those bounds we have o'erlooked,
And calmly run on in obedience,
Even to our ocean, to our great King John....
My arm shall give thee help to bear thee hence,
For I do see the cruel pangs of death
60 Right in thine eye....Away, my friends! New flight!
And happy newness, that intends old right.

                    [*they go, bearing Melun in their arms*

[5. 5.]   *The DAUPHIN's camp*

    LEWIS and his train return after the battle

    Lewis. The sun of heaven methought was loath to set,
But stayed, and made the western welkin blush,
When English measured backward their own ground
In faint retire: O, bravely came we off,

When with a volley of our needless shot,
After such bloody toil, we bid good night,
And wound our tattering colours clearly up,
Last in the field, and almost lords of it!

A Messenger hurries up

Messenger. Where is my prince, the Dauphin?
Lewis.   Here: what news?
Messenger. The Count Melun is slain; the English lords 10
By his persuasion are again fall'n off,
And your supply, which you have wished so long,
Are cast away and sunk on Goodwin Sands.
Lewis. Ah, foul shrewd news! beshrew thy very heart!
I did not think to be so sad to-night
As this hath made me....Who was he that said
King John did fly an hour or two before
The stumbling night did part our weary powers?
Messenger. Whoever spoke it, it is true, my lord.
Lewis. Well; keep good quarter and good care to-night. 20
The day shall not be up so soon as I,
To try the fair adventure of to-morrow.   [*they go*

[5. 6.]   *Near Swineshead Abbey; night*

The BASTARD *and* HUBERT, *meeting*

Bastard. Who's there? speak, ho! speak quickly, or
    I shoot.
Hubert. A friend....What art thou?
Bastard.   Of the part of England.
Hubert. Whither dost thou go?
Bastard. What's that to thee?
Hubert.   Why may not I demand
Of thine affairs, as well as thou of mine?

Bastard. Hubert, I think.

Hubert.   Thou hast a perfect thought:
I will upon all hazards well believe
Thou art my friend, that know'st my tongue so well:
Who art thou?

Bastard.   Who thou wilt: and if thou please,
10 Thou mayst befriend me so much as to think
I come one way of the Plantagenets.

Hubert. Unkind remembrance! thou and eyeless night
Have done me shame: brave soldier, pardon me,
That any accent breaking from thy tongue
Should 'scape the true acquaintance of mine ear.

Bastard. Come, come; sans compliment, what news
          abroad?

Hubert. Why, here walk I in the black brow of night
To find you out.

Bastard.   Brief, then; and what's the news?

Hubert. O, my sweet sir, news fitting to the night,
20 Black, fearful, comfortless, and horrible.

Bastard. Show me the very wound of this ill news—
I am no woman, I'll not swoon at it.

Hubert. The king, I fear, is poisoned by a monk.
I left him almost speechless, and broke out
To acquaint you with this evil, that you might
The better arm you to the sudden time,
Than if you had at leisure known of this.

Bastard. How did he take it? who did taste to him?

Hubert. A monk, I tell you, a resolvéd villain,
30 Whose bowels suddenly burst out: the king
Yet speaks and peradventure may recover.

Bastard. Who didst thou leave to tend his majesty?

Hubert. Why, know you not? the lords are all
          come back,
And brought Prince Henry in their company,

At whose request the king hath pardoned them,
And they are all about his majesty.
　Bastard. Withhold thine indignation, mighty heaven,
And tempt us not to bear above our power!
I'll tell thee, Hubert, half my power this night,
Passing these flats, are taken by the tide.　　　　　　　40
These Lincoln Washes have devouréd them.
Myself, well mounted, hardly have escaped....
Away before: conduct me to the king.
I doubt he will be dead or ere I come.　　　　*[they go*

[5. 7.]　　　*The orchard of Swinstead Abbey*

*PRINCE HENRY, SALISBURY and BIGOT
come from the abbey*

　P. Henry. It is too late! the life of all his blood
Is touched corruptibly: and his pure brain
(Which some suppose the soul's frail dwelling-house)
Doth by the idle comments that it makes
Foretell the ending of mortality.

PEMBROKE comes forth

　Pembroke. His highness yet doth speak, and
　　　　holds belief
That, being brought into the open air,
It would allay the burning quality
Of that fell poison which assaileth him.
　P. Henry. Let him be brought into the orchard here... 10
Doth he still rage?　　　　　　　*[Bigot goes within*
　Pembroke. 　　　　He is more patient
Than when you left him; even now he sung.
　P. Henry. O vanity of sickness! fierce extremes
In their continuance will not feel themselves.

Death, having preyed upon the outward parts,
†Leaves them invisible, and his siege is now
Against the mind, the which he pricks and wounds
With many legions of strange fantasies,
Which, in their throng and press to that last hold,
20 Confound themselves....'Tis strange, that death
       should sing:
I am the cygnet to this pale faint swan,
Who chants a doleful hymn to his own death,
And from the organ-pipe of frailty sings
His soul and body to their lasting rest.
    Salisbury. Be of good comfort, prince, for you are born
To set a form upon that indigest
Which he hath left so shapeless and so rude.

      Bigot returns with attendants carrying
           King John *in a chair*

    K. John. Ay, marry, now my soul hath elbow-room.
It would not out at windows nor at doors.
30 There is so hot a summer in my bosom,
That all my bowels crumble up to dust:
I am a scribbled form drawn with a pen
Upon a parchment, and against this fire
Do I shrink up.
    P. Henry.   How fares your majesty?
    K. John. Poisoned—ill fare: dead, forsook, cast off,
And none of you will bid the winter come
To thrust his icy fingers in my maw;
Nor let my kingdom's rivers take their course
Through my burned bosom; nor entreat the north
40 To make his bleak winds kiss my parchéd lips
And comfort me with cold....I do not ask you much,
I beg cold comfort; and you are so strait
And so ingrateful, you deny me that.

P. Henry. O, that there were some virtue in my tears,
That might relieve you!
    K. John.   The salt in them is hot....
Within me is a hell, and there the poison
Is, as a fiend, confined to tyrannize
On unreprievable condemnéd blood.

The Bastard enters in haste

Bastard. O, I am scalded with my violent motion,
And spleen of speed to see your majesty!   50
    K. John. O cousin, thou art come to set mine eye:
The tackle of my heart is cracked and burnt,
And all the shrouds wherewith my life should sail
Are turnéd to one thread, one little hair:
My heart hath one poor string to stay it by,
Which holds but till thy news be utteréd,
And then all this thou see'st is but a clod
And module of confounded royalty.
    Bastard. The Dauphin is preparing hitherward,
Where heaven He knows how we shall answer him: 60
For in a night the best part of my power,
As I upon advantage did remove,
Were in the Washes all unwarily
Devouréd by the unexpected flood.   *[the King dies*
    Salisbury. You breathe these dead news in as dead
        an ear.
My liege! my lord! but now a king, now thus.
    P. Henry. Even so must I run on, and even so stop!
What surety of the world, what hope, what stay,
When this was now a king, and now is clay!
    Bastard. Art thou gone so? I do but stay behind   70
To do the office for thee of revenge,
And then my soul shall wait on thee to heaven,
As it on earth hath been thy servant still....

[*to the nobles* Now, now, you stars, that move in your
      right spheres,
Where be your powers? show now your
      mended faiths,
And instantly return with me again,
To push destruction and perpetual shame
Out of the weak door of our fainting land:
Straight let us seek, or straight we shall be sought—
80 The Dauphin rages at our very heels.
    Salisbury. It seems you know not, then, so much
      as we.
The Cardinal Pandulph is within at rest,
Who half an hour since came from the Dauphin,
And brings from him such offers of our peace
As we with honour and respect may take,
With purpose presently to leave this war,
    Bastard. He will the rather do it, when he sees
Ourselves well sinewéd to our defence.
    Salisbury. Nay, it is in a manner done already,
90 For many carriages he hath dispatched
To the sea-side, and put his cause and quarrel
To the disposing of the cardinal:
With whom yourself, myself and other lords,
If you think meet, this afternoon will post
To consummate this business happily.
    Bastard. Let it be so. And you, my noble prince,
With other princes that may best be spared,
Shall wait upon your father's funeral.
    P. Henry. At Worcester must his body be interred,
100 For so he willed it.
    Bastard.   Thither shall it then.
And happily may your sweet self put on
The lineal state and glory of the land!
To whom, with all submission, on my knee

I do bequeath my faithful services
And true subjection everlastingly.
　Salisbury. And the like tender of our love we make,
To rest without a spot for evermore.
　P. Henry. I have a kind soul that would give
　　you thanks,
And knows not how to do it but with tears.
　Bastard. O, let us pay the time but needful woe,　　110
Since it hath been beforehand with our griefs....
This England never did, nor never shall,
Lie at the proud foot of a conqueror,
But when it first did help to wound itself....
Now these her princes are come home again,
Come the three corners of the world in arms,
And we shall shock them: nought shall make us rue,
If England to itself do rest but true.　　　　　　*[they go*

GLOSSARY

Note. Where a pun or quibble is intended, the meanings are distinguished as (*a*) and (*b*)

ABORTIVE (sb.), abortion, untimely or monstrous birth; 3. 4. 158

ABSEY BOOK, ABC book; 1. 1. 196

ABSTRACT (sb.), a compendium, 'a smaller quantity containing the virtue or power of a greater' (O.E.D. quoting Johnson); 2. 1. 101

ACCENT, a significant tone or sound; a word; 5. 6. 14

ACTION, gesture (cf. *Macb.* 5. 1. 32 'It is an accustomed action with her, to seem thus washing her hands'); 4. 2. 191

ADJUNCT TO, consequent upon; 3. 3. 57

ADVANCE (vb.), to move upward, raise (cf. *Temp.* 1. 2. 413); 2. 1. 207

ADVANTAGE, (i) interest (cf. *M.V.* 1. 3. 66–7); 3. 3. 22; (ii) opportunity; 3. 4. 151; (iii) 'upon advantage' = by stratagem or surprise, or on opportunity; 5. 7. 62

ADVENTURE (sb.), fortune, luck; 5. 5. 22

ADVICE, prudence, judgment; 3. 4. 11

ADVISED, (i) 'be well advised' = take thought; 3. 1. 5; (ii) well considered; 4. 2. 214

AERY, nest of a bird of prey; 5. 2. 149

AFFECT, take after, suggest; 1. 1. 86

AFFECTION, emotion, passion; 5. 2. 41

AGUE, malarial fever, especially the cold or shivering stage of an attack; 3. 4. 85

ALCIDES, Hercules; 2. 1. 144

ALMOST, even. 'Used to intensify a rhetorical interrogative' (O.E.D.), but also in other connexions (cf. *Temp.* 3. 3. 34; *Cor.* 1. 2. 24); 4. 3. 43

ALOFT (prep.), above (cf. 2 *Hen.VI*, 5. 1. 204; but not found elsewhere in Sh.); 4. 2. 139

AMAZED, stunned, confused; 2. 1. 226, 356; 4. 2. 137; 4. 3. 140

AMAZEMENT, bewilderment, distraction; 5. 1. 35

AMIABLE, lovable, worthy to be loved; 3. 4. 25

ANATOMY, skeleton (here personifying death); 3. 4. 40

ANGEL, a golden coin worth 10s., so called because one side represented the archangel Michael slaying the dragon; 2. 1. 590; 3. 3. 9

ANGERLY, with anger or resentment; 4. 1. 82

ANSWER (vb.), account for or atone for; 4. 2. 89

APISH, ape-like in manner, foolish; 5. 2. 131

APPARENT, manifest; 4. 2. 93

APPOINTMENT, equipment; 2. 1. 296

APT, ready and willing; 4. 2. 226

ARMADO, a fleet of warships; 3. 4. 2

ARRAS, the hangings of a room (they hung loose upon the wall so that there was space for a person to hide behind them as Polonius does in *Ham.* 4. 2); 4. 1. 2

ARTICLE, 'each of two distinct charges, or counts, of an accusation or indictment' (O.E.D.); 2. 1. 111

ARTIFICER, artisan; 4. 2. 201

ASSURANCE. Legal: the securing of a title to property, hence title or claim to anything; 2. 1. 471

ASSURED, (a) sure, (b) betrothed (cf. *Err*. 3. 2. 140 'I was assured to her'); 2. 1. 534, 535

ATÉ, the goddess of discord or mischief; 2. 1. 63

AVAUNT, lit. forward! hence begone! away! 4. 3. 77

AWELESS, fearless; 1. 1. 266

BABE, doll (cf. *Macb*. 3. 4. 106 'a baby of a girl'); 3. 4. 58

BANK (vb.), to skirt, sail past (v. note); 5. 2. 104

BASILISCO-LIKE, (v. note); 1. 1. 244

BASTINADO, beating, cudgelling; 2. 1. 463

BATED, lowered, abated; 5. 4. 53

BATTLE, an army in battle array; 4. 2. 78

BEADLE, a parish officer, whose duty it was to whip malefactors; 2. 1. 188

BEAR, carry out, execute; 3. 4. 149; 4. 2. 101

BEAT, drive back; 2. 1. 88

BECOME, (i) to befit; 2. 1. 141; (ii) to adorn, grace; 5. 1. 55

BEDLAM, lit. an inmate of Bethlehem Hospital for the insane, hence a lunatic; 2. 1. 183

BEFOREHAND (to be), to have money in hand, to draw money in advance (O.E.D. 1 d); 5. 7. 111

BEHAVIOUR, 'person'; 1. 1. 3

BEHOLDING, indebted, obliged; 1. 1. 239

BELDAM, old woman; 4. 2. 185

BENT, (i) aimed (borr. from archers, cf. 3 *Hen. VI*, 5. 1. 87; *Rich. III*, 1. 2. 95); 2. 1. 37; (ii) inclined; 2. 1. 422

BEQUEATH, bestow, give; 1. 1. 149; 5. 7. 104

BESHREW, a curse upon; 5. 4. 49

BESTOW ONESELF, conduct oneself; 3. 1. 225

BIAS, anything that causes something to turn or swerve from its direct course (a term of bowls); 2. 1. 574

BLOOD, (a) man of spirit, (b) stock; 2. 1. 278, 461

BLOODY, containing blood; 4. 2. 210

BLOT (sb.), blemish; 3. 1. 45

BLOT (vb.), calumniate, 'throw mud at' (Onions); 2. 1. 132

BOISTEROUS, painfully rough; 4. 1. 95

BOTTOM, a ship; 2. 1. 73

BOUGHT AND SOLD, betrayed; 5. 4. 10

BOUNCE (sb.), bang; 2. 1. 462

BOUND. enclose, confine; 2. 1. 431, 442

BOUNDEN, under obligation, indebted; 3. 3. 29

BRABBLER, brawler; 5. 2. 162

BRACED, stretched, made tense; 5. 2. 169

BRAVE (sb.), bravado; 5. 2. 159

BRAVE (vb.), (a) defy, (b) make a brave show upon; 5. 1. 70

BRAVELY, finely, splendidly; 5. 5. 4

BRAWL DOWN, to force down by brawling or noisy disturbance; 2. 1. 383

BREACH, rent, tear; 4. 2. 32

BREAK OUT, escape; 5. 6. 24

BREAK WITH, communicate with, confide in; 4. 2. 227

BREAKING, escaping; 5. 6. 14

BREATHE, utter; 3. 1. 256; 4. 2. 36

BREED (vb.), to be in the womb of the future; 3. 4. 170

BRIEF (sb.), note, summary, abstract; 2. 1. 103

BRIEF IN HAND, shortly to be dispatched (cf. *Rom.* 3. 3. 174 'brief to part'); 4. 3. 158

BROAD-EYED, all-seeing (v. note); 3. 3. 52

BROKER, a go-between; 2. 1. 568

BUSS, to kiss (v. note); 3. 4. 35

CALL (sb.), lit. the cry of a decoy bird, (hence) the decoy itself; 3. 4. 174

CANKER, ulcer; 5. 2. 14; 'cankersorrow,' sorrow like a canker worm; 3. 4. 82

CANKERED, malignant, spiteful; 2. 1. 194

CANON OF THE LAW, decree of God's law; 2. 1. 180

CAPABLE OF, impressible by, susceptible to; 2. 1. 476; 3. 1. 12

CARRIAGES, baggage, the portable equipment of an army; 5. 7. 90

CAUSE, quarrel; 3. 4. 12; 5. 2. 30

CENSURE (vb.), judge, estimate; 2. 1. 328

CENTURE, cincture, girdle (v. note); 4. 3. 155

CHAP, jaw; 2. 1. 352

CHECK (vb.), control, hold in check; 2. 1. 123

CHOICE, a picked company; 2. 1. 72

CHRISTENDOM (by my), lit. by my baptism, (hence) = as I am a Christian; 4. 1. 16

CHURLISH, (i) niggardly; 2. 1. 519; (ii) rude; 2. 1. 76; 3. 1. 303

CIRCUMSTANCE, detail, beating about the bush (cf. *Ham.* 1. 5. 127); 2. 1. 77

CLAP UP, conclude a bargain by clasping hands (cf. *Shrew*, 2. 1. 318 'Was ever match clapped up so suddenly?'); 3. 1. 235

CLEARLY, 'without obstruction from the enemy' (Collier; cf. O.E.D. 'clear' *a* 18); 5. 5. 7

CLIMATE, region of the sky; 2. 1. 344

CLIP, to clasp, encompass; 5. 2. 34

CLOSE (adj.), secret; 4. 2. 72

CLOSELY, secretly; 4. 1. 133

CLOUT, cloth, rag; 3. 4. 58

CLUTCH, clench (cf. *Meas.* 3. 2. 47); 2. 1. 589

COCKERED, pampered; 5. 1. 70

COIL (sb.), turmoil, fuss; 2. 1. 165

COLBRAND, a Danish giant defeated by Guy of Warwick; 1. 1. 225

COLD, dead; 3. 1. 105

COLDLY, calmly (cf. *Ado*, 3. 2. 121 'Bear it coldly but till midnight'); 2. 1. 53

COME IN, submit (O.E.D. 'come' 59 f. quotes Spenser, *State of Ireland*, 'to come in and submitt himselfe to her Majestie'); 5. 2. 70

COME OFF, leave the field of battle. Gen. in a good sense in Sh. (cf. *Cor.* 1. 6. 1 'We are come off like Romans' etc.); 5. 5. 4

COMMODITY, self-interest, expediency; 2. 1. 573

COMMON, not royal (although belonging to the nobility); 3. 1. 8

COMPANIES = company; 4. 2. 167

COMPOSITION, (i) frame, physical make-up (cf. *Rich. II*, 2. 1. 73 'Oh how that name befits my composition; Old Gaunt indeed'); 1. 1. 88; (ii) the settling of a disagreement by mutual arrangement and concession; 2. 1. 561

COMPOUND (vb.), to settle by mutual agreement; 2. 1. 281

CONCEIT, understanding; 3. 3. 50

7

CONCLUDE, be conclusive, settle a question (cf. *L.L.L.* 4. 2. 170 'the text most infallibly concludes it'); 1. 1. 127

CONDUCT (sb.), (i) escort; 1. 1. 29; (ii) command, 4. 2. 129

CONFINE (sb.), territory within frontiers; 4. 2. 246

CONFOUND, ruin, bring to nought, nullify; 4. 2. 29; 5. 7. 20, 58

CONFUSION, annihilation, destruction; 2. 1. 359; 4. 3. 152

CONJUNCTION, union in marriage (O.E.D. 2); 2. 1. 468

CONJURE, to entreat, beseech; 4. 2. 269

CONSCIENCE, 'a matter of conscience; something about which scruples are or should be felt' (O.E.D.); 4. 2. 229

CONTAGIOUS, foul, noisome, pestilential; 5. 4. 33

CONTENT (adj.), quiet, not uneasy; 3. 1. 42

CONTROL, CONTROLMENT, restraint, compulsion; 1. 1. 17, 20; 5. 2. 80

CONVERSION, change in status, elevation in rank; 1. 1. 189

CONVERTITE, convert (to an approved course); 5. 1. 19

CONVICTED, vanquished; 3. 4. 2

COOP (vb.), enclose for protection or defence (v. O.E.D. 2); 2. 1. 25

COPY, pattern, example; 4. 2. 113

CORRECT, punish; 2. 1. 87

CORRUPTIBLY, so as to be corrupted, subject to dissolution; 5. 7. 2.

COUNTERFEIT, a false coin; 3. 1. 99

COUNTY, count, earl (v. note); 5. 1. 8

COUSIN, kinsman; 3. 1. 339

COVETOUSNESS, inordinate ambition to do well; 4. 2. 29

CRACKER, (*a*) boaster, braggart, *b*) firecracker; 2. 1. 147

CREATE = created; 4. 1. 107

CRY AIM, encourage, applaud, abet. A term of archery (cf. *M.W.W.* 3. 2. 40); 2. 1. 196

CRY OUT UPON, to exclaim against; 5. 2. 19

CULL, to choose, select; 2. 1. 40, 391; 5. 2. 114

DATE (sb.), duration, term (cf. *Son.* 18. 4 'all too short a date'); 4. 3. 106

DEAD, deadly; 5. 7. 65

DEAR, heavy, grievous; 1. 1. 257

DECAY, destruction, downfall; 1. 1. 28

DECEIT, being deceived; 1. 1. 215

DEFY, reject, disdain; 3. 4. 23

DENOUNCE, (i) pronounce, promulgate; 3. 1. 319; (ii) proclaim; 3. 4. 159

DEPART WITH, part with, give up; 2. 1. 563

DIFFERENCE, (*a*) disagreement, quarrel; (*b*) a mark of distinction in heraldry; 3. 1. 238

DIFFIDENCE, mistrust, doubt; 1. 1. 65

DIM, dull, lustreless, pale; 3. 4. 85

DISCIPLINE, skill in military affairs; 2. 1. 39, 261, 413

DISHABIT, to dislodge; 2. 1. 220

DISPATCH, to make haste; 4. 1. 27

DISPITIOUS, pitiless; 4. 1. 34

DISPOSE (sb.), disposal; 1. 1. 263

DISPOSE (vb.), regulate, govern; 3. 4. 11

DISTEMPERED, (i) inclement; 3. 4. 154; (ii) vexed, angry; 4. 3. 21

DIVINELY, in a holy or pious manner; 2. 1. 237

DOGGED, currish, malicious; 4. 1. 129; 4. 3. 149

DOMINATION, dominion; 2. 1. 176

DOUBT (vb.), fear; 4. 1. 19; 4. 2. 102; 5. 6. 44

DOUBTFUL, full of fear, apprehensive; 5. 1. 36

DOUBTLESS, free from apprehension; 4. 1. 130

DRAW, (i) draw out, expand; 2. 1. 103; (ii) collect; 4. 2. 118; 5. 2. 113

DRAWN, disembowelled (a quibble); 2. 1. 504

DRIFT (sb.), shower, driving storm; 2. 1. 412.

DUB, to confer knighthood by striking the shoulder with a sword; 1. 1. 245

DUST, grain of dust; 3. 4. 128; 4. 1. 93

EASY, (i) ready; 1. 1. 36; (ii) slight; 3. 1. 207

EFFECT (sb.), purport, meaning; 4. 1. 38

ELSE, otherwise; 2. 1. 276; 4. 1. 108

EMBASSY, ambassadorial mission or message (cf. *Hen. V*, 1. 1. 95); 1. 1. 6, 99

EMBATTLED, drawn up in battle array; 4. 2. 200

EMBOUNDED, confined, contained; 4. 3. 137

ENDAMAGEMENT, injury, harm; 2. 1. 209

ENVENOM, lit. to poison, hence to treat with venom or bitterness; 3. 1. 63

ESTATE, power, authority; 4. 2. 128

ETERNAL, immortal; 3. 4. 18

EVEN, just; 3. 1. 233; 5. 2. 169; 5. 7. 12

EXAMPLE, parallel, precedent; 3. 4. 13

EXAMPLED BY, having as precedent; 4. 3. 56

EXCLAMATION, clamour, loud complaint; 2. 1. 558

EXERCISE (sb.), training, practice of manly accomplishments; 4. 2. 60

EXHALATION, meteor; 3. 4. 153

EXPEDIENT, speedy; 2. 1. 60, 223; 4. 2. 268

EXPEDITION, speed; 2. 1. 79

EXTEND, graciously show (like royalty); 4. 1. 120

EXTREME (sb.), great distress caused by cruelty or sickness; 4. 1. 108; 5. 7. 13

FAIR FALL, may good befall; 1. 1. 78

FAIR-PLAY, pertaining to the laws of chivalry, equitable conditions or conduct; 5. 1. 67; 5. 2. 118

FAITH, loyalty; 5. 7. 75

FALL FROM, to forsake; 3. 1. 320

FALL OFF, to withdraw from allegiance; 5. 5. 11

FALL OVER, to go over, desert; 3. 1. 127

FANTASIED, filled with fancies; 4. 2. 144

FARE (sb.), (*a*) condition, state, (*b*) food; 5. 7. 35

FAST AND LOOSE, a cheating game played by gipsies who beguiled simple folk of their money by getting them to bet whether a knot in a leather belt or kerchief was fast or loose (cf. *A. & C.* 4. 12. 28); 3. 1. 242

FAVOUR, (sb.), appearance; 5. 4. 50; permission; 2. 1. 422

FEARFUL, full of fear; 4. 2. 106

FEARFULLY, with fear; 4. 2. 74

FEATURE, shape or proportions of the body; 2. 1. 126; 4. 2. 264

FELL (adj.), (i) fierce, ruthless; 3. 4. 40; (ii) deadly; 5. 7. 9

FENCE (sb.), skill with the sword; 2. 1. 290

FETCH ABOUT, change the course of a ship to the other tack; 4. 2. 24

FIGURE (sb.), shape; 5. 4. 25

FIGURE (vb.), paint or engrave with figures; 5. 2. 53

FINE, (a) penalty, or sum paid as penalty for an offence, (b) end; 5. 4. 37, 38

FLEET (vb.), pass away from the body (cf. *M.V.* 4. 1. 135); 2. 1. 285

FLESH (vb.), lit. render an animal eager for prey by the taste of blood, (hence) initiate or inure to bloodshed (v. note); 5. 1. 71

FLOOD, sea; 3. 4. 1

FOND, enamoured; 3. 4. 92

FONDLY, foolishly; 2. 1. 258

FOOT, footing, status (O.E.D. 'foot' 24); 1. 1. 182

FORAGE (vb.), (a) raven, rove in search of prey (of a lion; cf. *L.L.L.* 4. 1. 90; *V.A.* 554; *Hen. V*, 1. 2. 109–10 'to behold his lion's whelp Forage in blood of French nobility'); (b) here, to go in search of the enemy; 5. 1. 59

FORCE PERFORCE, by violent means; 3. 1. 142

FORCED, involuntary, imposed by force; 4. 2. 98

FORETHOUGHT, predestined; 3. 1. 312

FORM (sb.), (i) due shape, order; 3. 4. 101; (ii) image; 4. 2. 256; 5. 7. 32

FORWEARY (vb.), tire out; 2. 1. 233

FROM, clear of; 4. 1. 86; 'from forth,' out of; 5. 4. 45

FRONT (sb.), forehead, face, here used for the whole person; 2. 1. 356

FULSOME, offensive, physically disgusting; 3. 4. 32

GALL (vb.), wound, scratch; 4. 3. 94

GAP OF BREATH, mouth; 3. 4. 32

GAWDS, toys; 3. 3. 36

GENERAL (adj.), comprehensive, far-reaching; 4. 3. 17

GET, to be begotten; 1. 1. 259

GIDDY, crazy; 3. 1. 292

GILT, smeared (as with gold paint); 2. 1. 316

GIVE OFF, relinquish; 5. 1. 27

GIVE US LEAVE. A polite way of asking to be left alone (cf. *Ham.* 2. 2. 170, note): 1. 1. 230

GIVE WAY, allow precedence, permit to pass (cf. *Ham.* 4. 6. 37; *Temp.* 1. 2. 185–6); 1. 1. 156; 2. 1. 324

GLISTER, to glitter, sparkle; 5. 1. 54

GO TO, come, come! (an exclamation expressing remonstrance); 4. 1. 97

GOD-A-MERCY = God reward you. An expression of thanks commonly used in reply to an enquiry after one's health by an inferior (Onions); 1. 1. 185

GOOD DEN = good even. A form of salutation used at any time after noon; 1. 1. 185

GOODS = good, well-being; 4. 2. 64

GRACIOUS, endowed with divine grace; 3. 4. 81

GREEN (sb.), grassy ground; 2. 1. 242

GRIEF, (a) grievance, (b) sorrow; 4. 3. 29, 30

GRIM, hard featured; 3. 1. 43

GROAT, thin silver fourpenny piece (cf. note 1. 1. 142–3); 1. 1. 94

GROSSLY, (i) with want of clear perception, stupidly; 3. 1. 163; (ii) flagrantly; 4. 2. 94

GUARD (vb.), to ornament, lit. to face with trimmings (cf. *M.V.* 2. 2. 154; *Ado*, 1. 1. 269); 4. 2. 10

HALF-FACE, profile. Cf. Harrington, *Oceana* (ed. 1771, p. 28) 'Unless we would draw him with a half-face.' Commonly used in reference to coins; I. I. 92

HALTING, wavering, shifting (cf. I *Kings* xviii. 21); 5. 2. 174

HARBOURAGE, shelter; 2. I. 234

HARNESSED, in armour; 5. 2. 132

HATCH (sb.), a half-door, the lower half of a divided door; I. I. 171; 'take the hatch,' to leap over the hatch; 5. 2. 138

HAVE IN REST, to possess quietly (v. O.E.D. 'rest' sb. I. 4c); 4. 2. 55

HAVOC, 'cry havoc' = give the signal for indiscriminate slaughter (cf. *Ham.* G. 'havoc'); 2. I. 357

HAZARDS (on the), among the chances; I. I. 119

HEAD (sb.), army, raised force; 3. I. 193 (quibblingly); 5. 2. 113

HEAT = heated; 4. I. 61

HEAVY, wicked (cf. *Ham.* 4. I. 12 'O, heavy deed'); 4. 3. 58

HEINOUS, (i) grievous, severe; 3. 4. 90; (ii) infamous, atrocious; 4. 2. 71; 4. 3. 56

HENCE, in the next world (cf. *Ham.* 3. 2. 221 'Both here and hence'); 4. 2. 89; 5. 2. 29

HIGH TIDE, high day, festival; 3. I. 86

HOLD (sb.), stronghold; 5. 7. 19

HOLD HAND WITH, be on equality with, match (O.E.D. on this passage); 2. I. 494

HOLD IN CHASE, pursue (a hunting term); I. I. 223

HOLP, helped; I. I. 240

HUMOROUS, fickle; 3. I. 119

HUMOUR, (i) disposition, temperament; 'unsettled humours' = restless, dissatisfied men; 2. I. 66; (ii) (*a*) mood, (*b*) physio-logical humour (v. note); 4. 2. 209; 5. I. 12; (iii) caprice; 4. 2. 214

HURLY, commotion; 3. 4. 169

IDIOT, jester, professional fool; 3. 3. 45

IDLE, crazy, mad; 5. 7. 4

IDLY, (i) by chance; 4. 2. 124; (ii) carelessly, indolently; 5. I. 72

IMAGINARY, imaginative; 4. 2. 265

IMPORTANCE, importunity; 2. I. 7

INDENTURE, contract, mutual engagement; 2. I. 20

INDIFFERENCY, impartiality, equity; 2. I. 579

INDIGEST (sb.), a shapeless mass; 5. 7. 26

INDIRECTION, a crooked course (cf. *Ham.* 2. I. 63); 3. I. 276

INDIRECTLY, wrongfully (cf. *Hen. V*, 2. 4. 94); 2. I. 49

INDUE, to supply (with); 4. 2. 43

INDUSTRIOUS, of set purpose, deliberate (v. note); 2. I. 376

INFECT, to affect, imbue; 4. 3. 69

INFER, prove, demonstrate (cf. 2 *Hen. IV*, 5. 5. 14); 3. ·. 213

INFORTUNATE = unfortunate; 2. I. 178

INGRATE, ungrateful, thankless; 5. 2. 151

INTELLIGENCE, secret service; 4. 2. 116

INTEREST, right, title (cf. I *Hen. IV*, 3. 2. 98 'interest to the state'); 4. 3. 147; 5. 2. 89

INTERROGATORIES, questions put to a witness under oath to answer truthfully; 3. I. 147

INTERRUPTION, hindrance, obstruction; 3. 4. 9

INVASIVE, invading; 5. I. 69

JADE, a sorry creature; 2. I. 385

JUST-BORNE, justly borne; 2. I. 345

KEEP (vb.), occupy (cf. 'keep' = lodge, in mod. Oxford or Cambridge); 3. 3. 45

KNOW, recognize; 2. 1. 364; 3. 4. 77, 88; 5. 2. 88

LAMENTABLE, expressing sorrow; 3. 1. 22

LEGITIMATION, legitimacy; 1. 1. 248

LEISURE (to stay one's), to wait until he is unoccupied, here to wait until the winds are idle; 2. 1. 58; 'at leisure,' without haste, not immediately; 5. 6. 27

LIABLE, (i) subject; 2. 1. 490; 5. 2. 101; (ii) suitable, apt (cf. *L.L.L.* 5. 1. 88–9 'The posterior of the day... is liable, congruent, and measurable for the afternoon'); 4. 2. 226

LIE ON, belong to, be incident to; 1. 1. 119

LIEN = lain; 4. 1. 50

LIEU OF (in), in return for; 5. 4. 44

LIKE (adj.), likely, probable; 3. 4. 49

LIKE (vb.), please; 2. 1. 533

LIMIT (vb.), to appoint, specify; 5. 2. 123

LINE (vb.), (*a*) furnish a lining to, (*b*) reinforce; 2. 1. 352

LINEAL, by right of descent (v. note); 2. 1. 85

LOVE (sb.), act of kindness; 4. 1. 49

LOVELY, lovable; 3. 4. 25

LUSTY, (i) cheerful, vigorous; 1. 1. 108; (ii) insolent, arrogant; 5. 2. 117

MAID, daughter; 5. 2. 154

MAIDEN (adj.), unstained with blood (by analogy with 'maiden sword' e.g. 1 *Hen. IV*, 5. 4. 134); 4. 2. 252

MAIN, ocean; 2. 1. 26

MAKE A HAZARD, to take a chance or try (at); 2. 1. 71

MAKE A STAND AT, to pause, stop short at; 4. 2. 39

MAKE NICE OF, to scruple to use; 3. 4. 138

MAKE UP, to advance (O.E.D. 96 n); 3. 2. 5

MAKE WORK, make slaughter; 2. 1. 407

MALICIOUS, fierce (v. O.E.D. 2 b); 2. 1. 314

MAN OF COUNTRIES, traveller; 1. 1. 193

MANAGE (sb.), government, administration (cf. *M.V.* 3. 4. 25 'the manage of my house'); 1. 1. 37

MATTER, (*a*) fuel (cf. *V.A.* 1162 'As dry combustious matter is to fire'), (*b*) arguments; 2. 2. 85

MAW, throat or stomach; 5. 7. 37

MEASURE (sb.), music accompanying a stately dance; 3. 1. 304

MEDICINE, remedy, curative treatment of any kind (cf. *Lear*, 4. 7. 26–7 'Restoration hang Thy medicine on my lips'); 5. 1. 15

MESS, originally a group of four persons dining from the same dishes, hence 'table'; 1. 1. 190

METEOR. Often = 'any atmospheric phenomenon,' but here clearly refers to meteors or comets (cf. *Rich. II*, 2. 4. 9 'And meteors fright the fixed stars of heaven'); 3. 4. 157

METROPOLIS, the seat of a metropolitan bishop, that is, a bishop having the oversight of the bishops of a province; 5. 2. 72

MEW UP, to confine, conceal. A mew was a cage for hawks; 4. 2. 57

MINION, darling, favourite (cf.
1 *Hen. IV*, 1. 1. 83 'sweet
Fortune's minion'); 2 1. 392

MISPLACED, occupying a wrong
place, (here) usurping; 3. 4. 133

MISTEMPERED, disordered, de-
ranged; 5. 1. 12

MODERN, ordinary, commonplace;
3. 4. 42

MODULE, a mere image or counterfeit; 5. 7. 58

MOE = more; 5. 4. 17

MORE (adj.), greater; 2. 1. 34

MORTAL, deadly; 3. 1. 259

MORTALITY, (i) death; 4. 2. 82;
(ii) life; 5. 7. 5

MOTION, impulse, inclination;
1. 1. 212; 4. 2. 255

MOUSE (vb.), worry as a cat does
a mouse, tear, bite; 2. 1. 354

MUSE (vb.), wonder, feel surprise
(cf. *Macb.* 3. 4. 85 'Do not muse
at me,'); 3. 1. 317

MUTINE, mutineer; 2. 1. 378

NATURE, natural affection, human-
ity (cf. *Ham.* G.); 4. 2. 256

No HAD = had not; 4. 2. 207

NUMBER, item in a list; 2. 1. 347

OBSERVATION, obsequiousness, paying court (cf. *Ham.* 3. 1. 157
'the observed of all observers');
1. 1. 208

OCCASION (sb.), (i) emergency;
2. 1. 82; (ii) course of events;
4. 2. 125; (iii) theme, argument; 4. 2. 62

OFFENCE, resentment; 3. 4. 180

OFFEND, harm; 3. 3. 65; 4. 1. 132

OFFER (vb.), to attempt to inflict
an injury, to essay, dare (v.
O.E.D. 5); 4. 2. 94

ONCE, in short (cf. *Cor.* 2. 3. 1
'Once, if he do require our
voices'); 1. 1. 74

OR ERE, before; 4. 3. 20

ORDER (sb.), arrangement, conditions; 5. 1. 67; 5. 2. 4

OUTFACE, browbeat, intimidate;
2. 1. 97; 5. 1. 49

OUTLOOK, overcome by looking,
stare down; 5. 2. 115

OVERLOOK, to look over, survey;
2. 1. 344

OVERTHROW (sb.), destruction of
body or mind (cf. O.E.D. 4);
5. 1. 16

OWE, to own, be the owner of;
2. 1. 109, 248; 4. 1. 123 (with
a quibble on 'owe' to be in
debt); 4. 2. 99

PAINFULLY, laboriously; 2. 1. 223

PAINTED, fictitious, unreal (cf.
Rich. III, 1. 3. 241 'Poor painted
queen'); 3. 1. 105

PARLE, a conference under a truce;
2. 1. 205, 226

PARLEY, to confer, treat; 4. 2. 238

PART = party; 2. 1. 359; 5. 6. 2

PARTS, abilities, talents; 3. 4. 96

PARTY, part, behalf; 1. 1. 34;
3. 1. 123

PASS (vb.), neglect, leave unnoticed;
2. 1. 258

PASSION, emotion, emotional state;
3. 3. 47

PASSIONATE, grieved, sorrowful;
2. 1. 544

PATTERN, precedent; 3. 4. 16

PAWN (sb.), pledge; 5. 2. 141

PEER O'ER (vb.), tower above, look
down upon (cf. 'overpeer' *Ham.*
4. 5. 99, *M.V.* 1. 1. 12); 3. 1. 23

PEEVISH, perverse, obstinate; 2. 1.
402

PEISED, poised, balanced; 2. 1. 575

PELL-MELL, at close quarters, hand
to hand; 2. 1. 406

PENCIL, paint-brush (cf. *L.L.L.*
5. 2. 43); 3. 1. 237

PEREMPTORY, determined; 2.1.454
PERFECT (adj.), without fault, correct; 5.6.6
PHILOSOPHY, natural philosophy, science (v. O.E.D. 3); 3.4.51
PICKED, (a) who has picked his teeth, (b) exquisite, dandified; 1.1.193
PLANK, ? floor (v. note); 5.2.140
PLOT (sb.), (i) spot, piece of ground (cf. *M.N.D.* 3.1.3 'This green plot'); 2.1.40; (ii) 'lay a plot,' prepare a plan; 3.4.146
PLUCK ON, to draw on, incite; 3.1.57
POLICY, diplomacy, political sagacity; 2.1.396
POTENT (sb.), potentate, power; 2.1.358
PRACTICE, scheming, machination; 4.3.63
PRACTISE, to plan, scheme, intend; 4.1.20
PRATE (sb.), prattle; 4.1.25
PRECEDENT, the original from which a copy is made; 5.2.3
PREPARATION, an armed force for attack or defence, an armament; 4.2.111
PRESENTLY, immediately; 2.1.538
PRIVATE (sb.), ? a confidential communication (v. note); 4.3.16
PRODIGIOUS, monstrous; 3.1.46
PRODIGIOUSLY, ominously; 3.1.91
PRODUCE (vb.), present. Legal word; 1.1.46
PROMOTION, preferment, office of distinction (cf. *Rich. III*, 1.3.80); 2.1.492
PROPER, handsome, well-made; 1.1.250
PROPERLY, exactly, in accordance with fact (O.E.D. 2); 2.1.514
PROPERTY (vb.), make a tool of, use as a chattel (cf. *Tw. Nt.* 4.2.92; *Tim.* 1.1.57); 5.2.79

PROVOKE, urge on; 4.2.207
PUISSANCE, an armed force; 3.1.339
PURE, clear; 5.7.2
PUT O'ER, to refer; 1.1.62
PYRENEAN, the Pyrenees; 1.1.203

QUALIFY, to moderate, mitigate; 5.1.13
QUANTITY, fragment (cf. *Shrew*, 4.3.112 'thou quantity, thou remnant'); 5.4.23
QUARTER, (keep good), to keep good watch (cf. *1 Hen. VI*, 2.1.63; *Err.* 2.1.108); 5.5.20
QUOTED, written down, noted; 4.2.222

RAGE (sb.), madness; 4.3.49
RAGE (vb.), to rave; 5.7.11
RAM UP, to block up; 2.1.272
RAMPING, violent, extravagant; 3.1.122
RANKED, drawn up in ranks; 4.2.200
RANKNESS, headstrong or rebellious course (also used of a river in spate in *V.A.* 71); 5.4.54
RATED, (a) assessed, (b) estimated at its true value, exposed; 5.4.37
REASON (vb.), speak (cf. *M.V.* 2.8.27); 4.3.29
REBUKE (vb.), to check, repress; 2.1.9
REDRESS, 'remedy for, or relief from, some trouble' (O.E.D.); 3.4.24
REFUSE (vb.), to disclaim, disown (cf. *Ado*, 4.1.183); 1.1.127
REGREET (sb.), a (return) salutation; 3.1.241
RELIGIOUSLY, (i) piously, in accordance with the principles of religion; 2.1.246; (ii) solemnly, ceremoniously; 3.1.140;

(iii) faithfully, scrupulously (perhaps with some sense of (i)); 4. 3. 73

REMEMBER, remind; 3. 4. 96

REMORSE, compassion, pity; 2. 1. 478; 4. 3. 50, 110

REPAIR (sb.), restoration to a sound condition; 3. 4. 113

RESOLVE (vb.), (i) to dissipate, dispel; 2. 1. 371; (ii) to melt, dissolve; 5. 4. 25

RESOLVED, resolute, determined; 5. 6. 29

RESPECT (sb.), (i) a consideration, something taken into account; 3. 1. 318; 5. 4. 41; (ii) regard, esteem; 3. 3. 28; 5. 2. 44; (iii) view, opinion; 3. 4. 90; (iv) consideration, reflexion; 4. 2. 214; (v) self-respect; 5. 7. 85

RESPECTIVE, respectful; 1. 1. 188

RETIRE (sb.), retreat; 2. 1. 253, 326; 5. 5. 4

REVOLT (sb.), a rebel; 5. 2. 151; 5. 4. 7

RHEUM, tears; 3. 1. 22; 4. 1. 33

RIDING-ROD, a thin switch or stick used in riding; 1. 1. 140

RIGHT (adv.), (i) properly; 2. 1. 139; 3. 1. 183; (ii) clearly; 5. 4. 60

RIGHT (sb.), right way, straight road; 1. 1. 170

ROBE, an enveloping garment, here used for skin; 2. 1. 141

ROUND (vb.), to whisper; 2. 1. 566

ROUNDURE, circuit; 2. 1. 259

RUB (sb.), obstacle, hindrance. A term from the game of bowls; 3. 4. 128

RUDE, (i) violent, barbarous; 4. 2. 240; 5. 4. 11; (ii) crude; 5. 7. 27

RUMOUR, clamour, tumult; 5.4.45

SAFETY, custody; 4. 2. 158

SANS, without; 5. 6. 16

SCAMBLE, to struggle (in order to get something), scramble; 4. 3. 146

SCATH, harm; 2. 1. 75

SCOPE, an instance of liberty or licence (v. note and O.E.D. 7 b); 3. 4. 154

SCORN AT, to treat with ridicule, mock; 1. 1. 228

SCROYLE, scoundrel, wretch. 'The conjecture that it is adopted from O.F. *escroele*, scrofulous sore, is not quite satisfactory as to form, and the assumed development of sense, though plausible, has no evidence' (O.E.D.); 2. 1. 373

SECONDARY (sb.), a subordinate; 5. 2. 80

SECURELY, confidently, without apprehension; 2. 1. 374

SEIZURE, grasp, hand-clasp; 3.1.241

SEMBLANCE, appearance or outward seeming; 4. 3. 4

SET (sb.), the number of points required to win a game or match (cf. *Tit. And.* 5. 1. 100 'As sure a card as ever won the set'); 5. 2. 107

SET (vb.), to close; 5. 7. 51

SET APART, set aside, repudiate; 3. 1. 159

SHADOW (sb.), reflexion (cf. *V.A.* 162 'his shadow in the brook'); 2. 1. 498

SHADOW (vb.), shelter, protect; 2. 1. 14

SHOCK (vb.), to throw troops into confusion. O.E.D. vb.² 3 quotes Grafton, *Chron.* II, 1364 (1568) 'The Countie Egmond...recharged...so terribly that he shokt all their battayle'; 5.7.117

SHREWD, evil, bad (cf. *M.V.* 3. 2. 244 'shrewd contents'); 5. 5. 14

SHROUD, sail-rope; 5. 7. 53

SIGHTLESS, unsightly; 3. 1. 45

SIGHTLY, pleasing to the sight; 2. 1. 143

SIGNED, marked out. Onions suggests that it may be an aphetic form of 'assigned'; 4. 2. 222

SINEWED, strengthened; 5. 7. 88

SIR NOB (v. note); 1. 1. 147

SKIN-COAT, (a) coat made of (lion's) skin, (b) his own skin; 2. 1. 139

SLANDEROUS, discreditable; 3. 1. 44

SMOKE ONE'S SKIN-COAT, give one a sound basting; 2. 1. 139

SOCIABLE, affable, companionable; 1. 1. 188; 3. 4. 65

SOLE, unique; 4. 3. 52

SOLEMNITY, wedding ceremony (cf. *M.N.D.* 1. 1. 11); 2. 1. 555

SOOTH, truth; 4. 1. 29

SOOTHE UP, flatter (Cf. Kyd. *S. Trag.* 3. 10. 19; Nashe, ii, 39); 3. 1. 121

SOUL-FEARING, inspiring fear in the very soul; 2. 1. 383

SOUND (vb.), to utter, express (cf. *Lucr.* 717; *Rich. II*, 3. 4. 75); 4. 2. 48

SOUSE (vb.), to swoop upon. A hawking term; 5. 2. 150

SPARKLE (vb.), to send out sparks; 4. 1. 115

SPEED (vb.), (a) to prosper, (b) to go with speed; 4. 2. 141

SPITE (in spite of), in spite of everything, do what we can; 5. 4. 5

SPLEEN, (i) the organ itself, regarded as the seat of ill-temper; 2. 1. 68; (ii) eagerness; 2. 1. 448 (v. note); 5. 7. 50; (iii) hot and hasty temper; 4. 3. 97

SPOT (sb.), disgrace; 5. 2. 30

SPRIGHTFUL, full of spirit; 4. 2. 177

STAFF, spear or lance; 2. 1. 318

STAND BY, to stand aside; 4. 3. 94

STARS, a person's fortune or destiny, viewed as determined by the stars; 3. 1. 126

STATE (sb.), (i) government as embodied in the ruler; 2. 1. 97; (ii) prince, ruler (cf. *Troil.* 4. 5. 65); 2. 1. 395; (iii) seat of state; 3. 1. 70; (iv) pomp; 4. 3. 147

STAY (sb.), (i) (a) check, set-back, (b) sudden check in horse riding (v. note); 2. 1. 455; (ii) support; 5. 7. 68

STAY (vb.), (i) await; 2. 1. 58; (ii) prop, hold up; 3. 4. 138; 5. 7. 55

STILL, constantly, always; 5. 7. 73; 'still and anon,' constantly from time to time (O.E.D.); 4. 1. 47

STORED, stocked, supplied; 5. 4. 1

STRAIGHT, straightway; 2. 1. 149; 4. 3. 22

STRAIT (adj.), stingy, close; 5. 7. 42

STRANGER, alien, foreign; 5. 1. 11

STUDY (sb.), solicitous endeavour; 4. 2. 51

STUMBLING, that trips up or overthrows (v. O.E.D. 'stumble' (vb.) 4); 5. 5. 18

SUBJECTED, submissive, obedient, perhaps with a play on being the king's subject; 1. 1. 264

SUDDENLY, instantly (cf. *Ham.* 2. 2. 214); 5. 6. 30

SUGGESTION, incitement, temptation; 3. 1. 292; 4. 2. 166

SUPERNAL, 'that is above or on high' (O.E.D.); 2. 1. 112

SUPPLY, a reinforcement of troops; 5. 3. 9; 5. 5. 12

SURETY, security; 5. 7. 68

SUSPIRE, to breathe; 3. 4. 80

SWART = swarthy; 3. 1. 46

SWAY (vb.), to rule; 2. 1. 344

SWINGE, to beat, flog; 2. 1. 288

TABLE, 'a board or other flat surface on which a picture is painted' (O.E.D.); 2. 1. 503

TAKE A TRUCE, make peace; 3. 1. 17

TAKE HEAD, to make a rush forward, start running; 2. 1. 579

TAKE IT (on his death), to affirm, swear (by his death); 1. 1. 110

TAME TO, submissive to; 4. 2. 262

TARRE, incite, provoke (to fight); 4. 1. 117

TASK (vb.), subject, compel; 3. 1. 148

TASTE (vb.), to act as taster, to certify the wholesomeness of food by tasting it; 5. 6. 28

TATTERING, ragged; 5. 5. 7

TEMPORIZE, come to terms; 5. 2. 125

TENDER (sb.), offer; 5. 7. 106

TERRITORY, dependency (v. note); 1. 1. 10

THREE-FARTHINGS, ? a paltry fellow (v. O.E.D.); 1. 1. 143

THRILL, shiver (cf. *Meas.* 3. 1. 122 'thrilling region of thick-ribbed ice'); 5. 2. 143

TICKLING, (i) flattering; 2. 1. 573; (ii) tingling. The regular word to describe 'a pleasantly tingling or thrilling sensation...of the heart, lungs, blood, "spirits"' (O.E.D. 'tickle' vb. 1). Cf. Spenser *Muiopotmos* 394 'Who...with secrete ioy...Did tickle inwardly in euerie vaine'; 3. 1. 44

TIDE, time, season; 3. 1. 86

TIME, the present state of affairs; the present regime; 4. 2. 61; 5. 2. 12; 5. 6. 26

TIMES, the future; 4. 3. 54

TITHE (vb.), to exact or collect tithes; 3. 1. 154

TO, in addition to; 1. 1. 144

TOLL (vb.), to exact or collect a tax; 3. 1. 154

TOOTH, appetite (v. note); 1. 1. 213

TOWER (vb.). A term in falconry; lit. 'to rise in circles till she reaches her "place"' Onions (cf. *Macb.* 2. 4. 12. 'A falcon towering in her pride of place'); hence, to soar; 2. 1. 350; 5. 2. 149

TOY, 'a piece of fun, amusement, entertainment' (O.E.D.); 1. 1. 232

TRADED, practised; 4. 3. 109

TRAIN (vb.), to draw on, allure; 3. 4. 175

TRANSLATE, interpret; 2. 1. 513

TREATY, proposal; 2. 1. 481

TRICK (sb.), trait; 1. 1. 85

TROTH, faith; 3. 3. 55; 4. 1. 104

TRUE, just; 4. 3. 84

TRUMPET, trumpeter; 2. 1. 198

TRUTH, honesty, virtue; 1. 1. 169; cf. 3. 1. 273, 283

UNACQUAINTED, unfamiliar, unknown; 3. 4. 166

UNADVISED, rash, indiscreet; 2. 1. 45 (with a play on 'without receiving news'); 2. 1. 191; 5. 2. 132

UNATTEMPTED, not tempted; 2. 1. 591

UNDER-BEAR, to endure, suffer; 3. 1. 65

UNDER-WROUGHT, undermined; 2. 1. 95

UNFENCED, undefended; 2. 1. 386

UNHAIRED, beardless; 5. 2. 133

UNOWED, unowned; 4. 3. 147

UNREVEREND, irreverent; 1. 1. 227

UNSURED, uncertain; 2. 1. 471

UNTOWARD, indecorous, unseemly; 1. 1. 243

UNTREAD, to retrace; 5. 4. 52

UNTRIMMED, with the hair hanging down after the fashion of brides (cf. note); 3. 1. 209

UNVEXED, unmolested; 2. 1. 253

UNWARILY, without warning, un-
expectedly; 5. 7. 63

UNYOKE, to unlink, disjoin;
3. 1. 241

UPON, against; 3. 1. 193

VAULTY, having the form of a
hollow arch; 3. 4. 30; 5. 2. 52

VEIN, (a) blood-vessel, (b) mood,
humour (cf. *Err.* 2. 2. 20 'this
merry vein'); 5. 2. 38

VILE-DRAWING, attracting towards
evil; 2. 1. 577

VISIT (vb.), to punish; 2. 1. 179

VOLQUESSEN, 'the ancient country
of the Velocasses, whose capital
was Rouen; divided in modern
times into Vexin Normand and
Vexin Française' (Wright);
2. 1. 527

VOLUNTARY (sb.), a volunteer;
2. 1. 67

VOUCHSAFE, to condescend to
accept; 3. 1. 294

VULGAR, common to all; 2. 1. 387

WAFT, to convey safely by water;
2. 1. 73

WAIST, girdle; 2. 1. 217

WALL-EYED, lit. having the iris
of the eye discoloured, (hence)
having glaring eyes (cf. *Tit. And.*
5. 1. 44, Spenser, *F.Q.* 1. 4. § 24
'whally eyes (the signe of gelosy),'
and Marston, *Insat. Countess*, l. 1
'wall-ey'd Ielousie'); 4. 3. 49

WANTON (sb.), a spoilt child;
5. 1. 70

WANTON (adj.), frivolous; 3. 3. 36

WANTONNESS, whim, sport; 4. 1. 16

WARN, to summon; 2. 1. 201

WEAL, welfare; 4. 2. 65

WEATHER, storm, rain; 4. 2. 109

WELKIN, the vault of heaven, the
sky; 5. 2. 172

WHAT THOUGH? what matter?
1. 1. 169

WHEREUPON, to the degree that;
4. 2. 65

WHET ON, to urge on; 3. 4. 181

WILD, agitated; 5. 1. 35

WILDLY, distractedly; 4. 2. 128

WILFUL-OPPOSITE, obstinate; 5. 2.
124

WIN OF, get the better of, win
from by underhand means;
2. 1. 569

WIT, understanding; 3. 4. 102

WITHAL, (i) therewith; 2. 1. 531;
(ii) with; 3. 1. 327

WORSHIP, a distinction or dignity
(v. O.E.D. 3 b); 4. 3. 72

WRACK = wreck; 3. 1. 92; 5. 3. 11

YET, as yet; 2. 1. 361; 4. 3. 91

ZEAL, religious fervour; 2. 1.
565

ZEALOUS, fervent, religious; 2. 1.
428

'ZOUNDS = God's wounds; 2. 1.
466